PROS AND CONS

How Authors Can Make the Most
of a Convention Appearance

PROS AND CONS

How Authors Can Make the Most of a Convention Appearance

JODY LYNN NYE & BILL FAWCETT

WordFire Press
Colorado Springs, Colorado

PROS AND CONS
Copyright © 2016 Bill Fawcett & Associates

All rights reserved. No part of this book may be reproduced or transmitted in any form or by any electronic or mechanical means, including photocopying, recording or by any information storage and retrieval system, without the express written permission of the copyright holder, except where permitted by law.

The authors and publisher have strived to be as accurate and complete as possible in creating the Million Dollar Writing series. We don't believe in magical outcomes from our advice. We do believe in hard work and helping others. The advice in our Million Dollar Writing series is intended to offer new tools and approaches to writing. We make no guarantees about any individual's ability to get results or earn money with our ideas, information, tools or strategies. We do want to help by giving great content, direction and strategies to move writers forward faster. Nothing in this book is a promise or guarantee of future book sales or earnings. Any numbers referenced in this series are estimates or projections, and should not be considered exact, actual or as a promise of potential earnings. All numbers are for the purpose of illustration. The sole purpose of these materials is to educate and entertain. Any perceived slights to specific organizations or individuals are unintentional. The publisher and authors are not engaged in rendering legal, accounting, financial, or other professional services. If legal or expert assistance is required, the services of a competent professional should be sought.

ISBN: 978-1-61475-498-5

Cover design by Janet McDonald
Cover artwork images by Adobe Stock
Kevin J. Anderson, Art Director
Book Design by RuneWright, LLC
www.RuneWright.com

Published by
WordFire Press, an imprint of
WordFire, Inc.
PO Box 1840
Monument CO 80132

Kevin J. Anderson & Rebecca Moesta, Publishers

WordFire Press Trade Paperback Edition December 2016
Printed in the USA
wordfirepress.com

Contents

How to be a Literary Guest at a Convention	1
Choosing Who and Where?	15
Doing Business at a SF Con	35
Small Conventions	51
Practical Tips for Moderating a Panel	67
Book Signings	79
Writer's Workshops	91
Attending Gen Con	105
Shared Experiences	111

HOW TO BE A LITERARY GUEST AT A CONVENTION

These articles are designed to advise an author, potential author, editor, artist or even illustrator attending Science Fiction conventions on how to get the most from them. They include advice from many bestselling authors and editors along with our own. This book is a collection of articles that appeared in the SFWA Bulletin. If you are a new writer or aspire to be one, you are encouraged to join SFWA or at least get a subscription to their Bulletin.

You are a newly minted professional writer. One of the best ways to get to know your fans and attract potential readers is to attend conventions. There you would be on panels and workshops, sign books and talk with a targeted population who are intensive consumers of science fiction and fantasy literature such as yours.

How can you get to be on the program schedule? Reach out to the convention of your choice. Do you know someone on the committee? SF conventions have a hierarchy but it is relatively flat compared to most other organizations. Steven Silver, who has been convention chair and director of programming for Windycon and Chicon, suggests writing to the head of programming for the coming year. The names and e-mail links of committee members are usually listed on the convention website. If you wish to be in the current year's convention, it may be too late to be listed in the advertising (flyers on the table already printed), but you can get into the online listings, and you can still attend and participate.

An established convention will probably have someone in mind for its guest of honor spots already, but they might be interested in you as a featured guest or program participant. (That is not to say that new pros have not been made GoH, but that is a rarity, usually as a result of having had a very high profile publication release.) Your aim is to convince them that you are just the person they need on the schedule.

Asking to be a program participant is very much a job interview. What do you have to offer this convention besides your one book, story or poem? How can you make the convention experience more fun for the attendees? What value do you have beyond the fact that you have persuaded someone to pay you for your writing? Do you have special expertise? Can you run a writers' workshop? Do you do any martial arts? Can you demonstrate or teach a skill of interest to the fans? Do you have a slide show of your work? Do you filk? Will you do Young Adult programming (a *big* new draw)? There are a lot of new writers out there. What sets you apart from the others? Steven Silver suggests that you come to the committee with ideas on how it can use you.

In most cases, no special additional skill is needed. Con-coms need to fill up their program schedule, and it simply adds value to the program to feature multiple professional writers (it takes pressure off the GoH). The easiest way to appeal to the committee is to live near the convention venue. Many conventions have a sense of regional pride and want to promote their local writers. (For example, according to its bylaws, Westercon's GoH must live in the states that comprise its territory.) If you are local, it makes you more attractive to the con-com, because they won't have to pay travel expenses. The closer you live, the smaller the outlay they must make to have you. Carl Fink, Director, Panel Programs, for I-CON in Long Island, New York, says that I-CON is happy to have any local pros get in touch regarding future conventions. It is not a guarantee of an invitation to appear. What would tip the balance in your favor is how many unique paying members you can draw to the con.

That said, this is a negotiation. You have needs as well. This is an opportunity for you to meet your public and gain readers and friends in the broader SF community. The least you should hope for in return for your participation is a free membership for you or you and a guest. You are giving up an entire weekend of potential earning time for a non-paying appearance. The minimum outlay a convention would make on your behalf is for a badge, a copy of the program book and a pocket program flyer. The committee is already printing those for the rest of the membership; to increase the print run by one for you is a minimal expense.

You add value far above that. You're not taking up any extra function space or electricity. Still, be humble and see the situation from the point of view of the committee. It is a matter of economics, and con-runners must keep to a budget. The cheaper you are to bring in and the easier you are to cope with, the better. If the convention really wants you, but money is tight (and it always is), you may be able to negotiate for partial support, such as half your airfare, or a hotel room but no travel expenses. You can always ask, but be reasonable in your demands.

Still, some conventions require everyone from the guest of honor down to the last gofer to pay a membership fee to defray expenses. There are events in which this is the norm, such as the World Fantasy Convention^{SM} or the World Science Fiction Convention, because of the enormous cost of putting on those conferences. In other cases, the convention requires a non-GoH to buy a membership fee up front to be reimbursed later. This often comes about if that con has been burned more than once by participants who accepted a free membership, then failed to show up for their panels. If paying up front is the tradition for a particular convention, accept it if you want to go. Long-running conventions have their policies spelled out somewhere on their websites. For example, Windycon, the largest Chicagoland regional, has five categories of guest listed on its site. As a newcomer, you will likely fall into the last-named group, "panelist." Dragon Con has panelists, pros, and special guests.

Small conventions may not be able to give you more than a badge at first, but as they grow they will look back on the participants who helped make their convention a success.

Leave them with a good impression. As you grow in importance, you may be offered more, but only if you were a good guest to begin with.

Steven Silver said that it irks committees when writers get in touch and demand to be placed on at least three panels, so the convention will be "deductible." The committee doesn't care about your tax situation. Making your outlay legitimate to the IRS is not why they invite you; in any case, the convention will be deductible as a professional expense whether or not you are on panels. It simply won't be as useful to you as a public appearance if you aren't.

If you are selected to participate in programming, you have duties to the convention, the committee that is sponsoring you, and fandom in general. Here are some guidelines to keep in mind.

Be personable

You are a professional guest, in that you are trading your participation for a consideration, to include such items as membership, housing, food, transportation, and possibly an honorarium (rare but beautiful). You owe your host committee and the convention your best behavior. When you arrive at the convention, introduce yourself to the committee. Let them know who you are.

Get to know the fans. They are why you are there. Just answering a few questions—feel free to deflect anything that makes you uncomfortable—gives the fans a personal connection that will last for years. Can you hold an audience? Can you walk that line between monopolizing a conversation and being a wallflower?

Do not build a wall of your publications between you and your public. Most con-runners whom I consulted hate it when writers bring copies of everything they have ever written and set them up in a row on the panel table. When you introduce yourself, the most you should do is hold up your current book or magazine and say what it is and where it can be obtained. Let the audience seek you out later if they want to know more. When you are on a panel, they want to see you, not your covers.

Mingle. Browse the con suite, open to the general membership, rather than the Green Room, which is reserved for program participants and committee members. Get to know people. If you find you can't get all the way up the hall without being stopped at least three times for conversations, you're doing it right.

Be professional

In your exalted position as published writer, your words and actions have more impact than those of another fan. Carry yourself as if everything you do is being recorded on video. Cooperate. Don't start arguments with fans. Don't be petty. (Discourse on panels is good; personal attacks, bad). If a fan threatens or stalks you, inform the con-com immediately. Handling problems is their job. Don't put yourself in personal danger, but don't be the cause of the dispute, either.

Dress professionally. For example, wearing a belly-dancer costume to your panels, unless your book is about belly-dancing, gives the wrong impression. You don't have to wear a suit or a dress, but control your attire. Once you are a very big name, you can do what you like, but not until then if you want to be taken seriously.

Watch your speech, at the convention and afterwards, online and in person. If you diss other conventions to the con-com you want to impress, they will wonder in private what you are saying about theirs. If you diss the convention that invited you, chances are poor that you will be invited back. You can say more among fellow pros, especially where the conversation is not recorded or forwardable, than you ever should in public.

Be sensible

Please control your relationship with alcohol or other substances. It is common for newcomers to throw off the constraints of social behavior in a seemingly permissible situation, but it looks bad for any guest, from neo-pro to SFWA Grand Master, to get stinking drunk at a convention. Also control your impulses with regard to other relationships, such as casual overnight encounters. It's not anyone's business to police your love life, but be discreet, considerate and legal. As noted above, your behavior carries more weight than a paying attendee. Perhaps you don't feel you ought to be taken as a role-model, but you already are.

If you have a medical condition that requires attention, special equipment, certain requirements in terms of a quiet/non-smoking/wheelchair-accessible hotel room, or you need a particular diet, please let the con-com know. They wish to please their guests, and will go to great efforts to oblige. Do not assume that they are aware of your needs. Especially make certain someone is aware if you have an incapacitating condition. There are so many reasons why someone might collapse unconscious on the floor, but if the paramedics are aware in advance whether to administer insulin or a clot-buster it can make the difference in saving your life.

Be interesting

If you are not a good public speaker, do a reading. If you are shy, let the program director know you'd rather be on panel discussions with a good moderator who can draw out limited answers from you. Let the attendees get to know a little something about you. That is why they have come. If all they wanted to know was your writing, they'd stay home and read. SF is such an interactive community that these personal encounters mean a lot.

Be prompt

The panel starts at 10:00 AM. Be there. Unless you have an emergency (or the venue is too spread out for realistic perambulation), be in your seat by the time the bell rings. As I mentioned above, your free membership is dependent upon your participation in a minimum number of events. Certainly your possibility of being invited back will depend on whether you show up at the items for which you are scheduled. According to all the con-runners that I consulted, this is a deal-breaker. Missing your program items violates the agreement you made with the convention. Programming doesn't want to have to check up on you. They assume, as a professional, that you will be where you say you will be, when you are expected to be there.

Be prepared

If you receive your program schedule before the convention, study it. Do you need to bone up on a subject? Do whatever it takes to be well-informed and well-spoken. If the subject listed is unfamiliar, read up on it. Remind yourself of the details. Bring notes. We're the nerds; flaunt your over-preparedness proudly. Don't insult the audience by sitting like a lump. They get to be the oil painting, not you.

Do you need a piece of special equipment for your presentation? Communicate in advance with the committee to make sure they have one or can accommodate yours. Check again with Operations when you arrive at the convention center. Have you volunteered for a reading? Bring your manuscript. No kidding: I once arrived at a convention and realized the book from which I had intended to read was sitting on the bed where I had been packing my suitcase. I was lucky that time; I was able to borrow a copy of it from the bookseller in the dealers' room. The shock made me concentrate on never doing that again.

Bring contact information for your fans, especially if you have a signing. Have you got a website? (You MUST have a website.) Do you have a Facebook page? Do you

Twitter? Do you have bookmarks or other giveaways? Let people know how to find you. Because you are new, this may be the first time most fans have ever seen your name. Help them to remember it when book-buying time comes around. If you know that there are booksellers in the dealer's room, get in touch to say you will be coming and ask if they can order your books. If they cannot obtain any in time, bring a few to sell.

Carl Fink has an excellent practical suggestion for neo-pros: memorize your one-minute biography. Not only will it give the tongue-tied something to say on a panel, but it will give the moderator information to build on when framing questions. You can also use it, Carl quipped, if you happen to get on an elevator with the editor of *Analog*.

Be flexible

You're intelligent enough to be a writer. If you are assigned to a panel on a subject with which you're unfamiliar, be the one who asks leading questions of the panelists who do know about it. If the subject is too far out there and you all find yourselves looking at one another in bemusement, wing it. If the subject is downright offensive, ask to be taken off that panel. We're there to be entertainment. If the audience has had a good time, you'll be a success. Regina Kirby, who has worn many hats for Dragon Con and Chattacon, including program director and con-chair, insists that if you have a problem or a time conflict, tell Programming as soon as possible when you receive your schedule, so they can replace you and proper notice can be given to the attendees.

On the flipside, can you step in if someone else has to miss an event? The committee will be grateful if you are willing to volunteer. Steven Silver pointed out that the powers that be will remember that positively in future years when your name comes up.

Be patient

The con-com, except in rare circumstances, is an all-volunteer army. Do not expect perfect organization, or that the person in a certain vital job will be ideal or even prepared for that job. Some con-coms have been in existence for decades and run their conventions to a standard that the Army would envy. Others don't. The hotel is not under the control of the committee. I've heard, even witnessed, horror stories of convention function rooms being co-opted by the hotel for an event they knew they were hosting (such as a wedding) but didn't bother to inform the convention. The committee may threaten to sue, but there is really nothing they can do but scramble to re-house the displaced events. They are doing the best that they can. You gets what you gets. Don't become part of their problems.

Be courteous

Do not overwhelm a panel that you are on by interrupting or cutting out a quieter participant whom the fans have come to see. A few years ago, Bill Fawcett was a moderator on a panel with the noted Hal Clement and a young, exuberant female writer who interrupted Clement every time he spoke. The impression on the audience was not positive. Sure, you will be nervous and want to make an impression. Wait your turn, speak to the point, and give the big-name pro that everyone else has come to see the chance to speak. You will get your opportunity.

Be grateful

Who was it that invited you or sponsored you to the convention? Be cognizant that he or she put his reputation on the line to fight for you in committee meetings. Thank them in person, by e-mail, with a note, a beer or with a gift such as a copy of your book. Remember also that science fiction is a small community, and it communicates incessantly (often *during* panels these days—you can find yourself being Twittered or blogged as you speak). If you behave in a jerk-like fashion, expect to have the word spread. The Internet never forgets. Neither do con-runners and fans. Treat them with respect. If you get a reputation for being friendly and helpful, you will move up the ladder from a casual panelist to a paid-for guest.

* * *

Dragon Con's Regina Kirby wants you to remember that many, if not most, of the fans that you are coming in contact with at a convention have never met you before. "First impressions are lasting. As are last. Getting a reputation as 'difficult' (to put it nicely) will not get you invited to many conventions. *Convention committees talk to one another.*" For better or for worse, the impression you make as a convention guest will last a lifetime. The con-runners with whom I spoke had some private (and rather juicy) stories of crash-and-burn guests, most of whom will never make their invitee list again. As Carl Fink pointed out, horror stories are a lot more fun to tell than "nothing-bad-happened" stories. Among them:

> The big-name pro who at the convention banquet publicly insulted the con-com member *who had invited him*, then behaved badly to the rest of the committee the remainder of the evening.

> Neo-pros who demand "don't you know who I am?" (This particular phrase ticked off all the con-runners I asked.)

> Neo-pros who ask for ridiculous considerations, such as first-class airfare for them and their entire entourage, on the strength of their solo self-published book.

> The science guest who invaded a panel and was warned off by the moderator, whom the science guest then made as if to punch, in full view of the audience. The moderator was in a wheelchair.

> Those guests who depart early from the convention before finishing their panels, and especially those who do not inform the con-com that they are leaving.

I realize how obvious most of the above information seems, but all of it has come from long-time con-runners who have seen it all and wished it hadn't happened on their watch.

Other guidelines are available for program participants. In the 1980s, Susan Shwartz published an excellent and more extensive article than this in the *SFWA Handbook*. It has been reprinted in the special edition of *Argentus, The Art of the Con* (www.sfsite.com/ ~silverag/argentus.html), Steven Silver's zine, in which you will find other insights on how a convention is put together, including the Minicon Moderator's Guidelines.

If all else fails, ask an experienced fellow panelist for guidance. Use common sense.

And enjoy yourself!

Choosing Who and Where?

This is perhaps the most basic decision a writer has to make: which conventions to attend and why. Literally hundreds of Science Fiction conventions are held every year. Beyond an interest in Science Fiction topics, they vary widely from a few dozen students in college clubs to major regions such as DeepSouthCon and Balticon, to massive shows such as Dragon Con and the World Science Fiction Convention. Many authors have made excellent use, often consciously, of conventions to further their writing careers. Back in the late 80s some marketing research was done that still is relevant today. It showed that about 80% of all science fiction books were purchased by just 20% of the book buyers. More than half of that 80% were purchased by the 5% that read two to three books a week. If you eliminate the books that are based on TV and movies, that 5% that buys a whole lot of books are also those who attend science fiction conventions.

A bit of a confession. The original intention was to write a long column full of check lists and wry observations. But then we asked for some comments from other authors whom we could quote. Considering the combined total writing talent of those from whom we asked for input, it became quickly apparent they were already saying it all too well to need to be rephrased.

Some conventions are "relaxacons" with small attendance and a relaxed, chatty atmosphere. Others are regional or larger local cons with hundreds of attendees and more regular programming. But these too can feature a widely different feel. To use just one example, let us look at the Chicago region. In the Windy City (named for its politicians, by the way, not its weather), you can find the largest, Windycon, with a traditional format and established committee, Duckon, with quirkier programming and emphasis on family-friendly programming and science; and Capricon, a good general con but that is also known for asking pros to pay to attend. There are also several smaller conventions such as MuseCon, a few media shows like Wizard Con and Chicago Comic Con. If that is the list for just one Midwestern city, how do you decide which conventions to attend and why? Rather than express our own opinions, we have asked a number of experienced professionals we have seen benefit from attending conventions three questions: What factors do you consider when deciding to attend a con, what would discourage you from attending a convention, does size matter, and why choose one convention over another?

First we asked the authors and editors to share what is the most important factor or factors that helps you to decide on whether to attend a convention?

We begin with Todd McCaffrey who, as the son of Anne McCaffrey, and now a best-selling author in his own right, has literally been attending conventions all of his life.

> I suppose the biggest factor is how much people want to see me. If I'm going to a convention where it's like "park him over in the field with the rest of the pros" then I'm a lot less likely to want to go than to a convention that says, "Ohmigosh! We're so happy to have you, is there anything we can do to convince you to come? How can we make your stay more enjoyable?"

Rob Sawyer has won both a Hugo and Nebula awards, and his novel was made into the ABC-TV series *FlashForward*.

> The convention's focus. Setting aside giant cons, like Dragon Con and San Diego Comic-Con, where there's plenty of room for everyone, if a smaller convention is mostly hyping its media or gaming aspects, I generally give it a miss. The fact is that there tend to be very few readers at such events, and although I sometimes do media-oriented panels, either on personal passions such as *Planet of the Apes* or on my experiences working on the TV adaptation of my novel *FlashForward*, for the most part there's really no upside in trying to convince those who are more interested in actors who played security guards on *Star Trek* that they should read a book.

Janny Wurts has a different perspective, being both a talented author and artist.

> If it looks like it will be fun, if it seems to center around our primary interests, if we feel we can contribute in a good way, and if it isn't on top of dates we've already committed. We do check to be sure it has a good reputation, and that both guests and attendees are well treated.

Mike Resnick has more Hugo nominations (and awards) than most of us have books published. He is this year's GoH at Chicon 7, and takes a more practical view.

> I go to so many that, other than WorldCon and WFC, the operative question these days is: will they comp my room and travel expenses?

Lynn Abbey has been a creative force in Science Fiction who, among other accomplishments, co-created the shared world anthology, in the early 1980s with *Thieves' World*. Like Mike Resnick and so many of us, she, too, takes a practical view.

> Cost first, followed by distance, which is usually related to cost.

Chelsea Quinn Yarbro has been a top seller and has been writing one of the first vampire series, Saint-Germain, for over three decades. She has attended conventions for even longer from WorldCons to vampire literature gatherings in Romania.

> The orientation of the convention is my primary factor; is the convention in any way addressing my professional strengths, and will I have a chance to display those strengths? For that reason, I probably wouldn't attend a convention dedicated to Harry Potter or one focused on violent computer games, because I have almost nothing to contribute and no opportunity to make the most of what I'm known for. One of the reasons I find Dragon Con valuable is it gives me opportunities to play to more than one strength, and to be accessible to those readers and fans new to my work.

Kevin J. Anderson is one of the most successful and creative authors in our genre. He is best known for his *Dune* and *Star Wars* novels. Always a great guest, after being featured at literally dozens of shows he takes a personal view.

> I go to a lot of conventions: some of them because I've attended previously, had a great time, and want to go back; others because they are in an area of the country I have not visited, so I get to meet (and hopefully make) a new set of fans. The schedule is also important, depending on whether I'm promoting a new book, or whether I'm exhausted from traveling. And friends, fans, con staff, all have an influence.

Kerrie Hughes has attended many shows both as an author and with her editor husband. So she looks at conventions from two directions.

> Other than the theme of the convention in general, i.e. Sci-Fi, Steampunk, World Fantasy, it comes down to price, distance, hotel, access to professionals and fans, and when it's scheduled.

John Helfers is an author who has written numerous genre and mainstream novels. He was also an editor for Tekno Books and over the last decade worked with almost every author in the field.

> Whether I was attending as an editor for Tekno or as a freelance editor, my goal is still the same: to meet with editors and authors and find out what's happening in publishing across the country. Therefore, the other attendees list is often the first thing I look at. Second is the programming list, both as a participant and attendee. Fresh, unusual programming is also a draw.

We also asked two well-known and established editors, Toni Weisskopf and Melissa Singer, for their insights. Their reasons and goals reflect their responsibilities.

Toni Weisskopf started as an editor at Baen Books in the mid-eighties and is now its publisher.

Guests of Honor—if there are Baen authors; or if a lot of my friends are going to go. Convention reputation is important. I also try to make sure I hit several regions of the country each year, and I look for new conventions that I haven't yet attended.

Melissa Singer has been editing at TOR Books and representing them at conventions for more than two decades. Much in her comprehensive answer can apply to both an editor or an author.

> Roughly in order of importance: If authors I am interested in will be attending—either authors I am working with or authors I would like to work with or just to get to know better. If agents I am interested in will be attending, especially if the convention is in a part of the country I don't visit often; it can be a good way to meet a number of agents in one place at one time. If the convention has a theme or topic focus which aligns with books I am editing or in which I am personally interested (often the same thing, but not always). If I have personal reasons to want to visit the city in which the convention will take place (family or close friends in the area; college of interest to my teenager; something/ someplace cool that I've always wanted to visit). Timing—it's hard to go to events too close to the beginning or end of the school year, to major Jewish holidays, to standing

family commitments, or to already-scheduled work events or other conferences/conventions.

One of the most important factors in deciding which convention to attend is what do you want from going? Is it to meet people, get feedback from a few fans, make a splash, or meet an editor? Going to a convention that can't fulfill your needs can be an expensive and frustrating experience.

Todd McCaffrey

What I saw that worked best for me when I was fan was the panels where the authors made me laugh, where I got the impression "this is a nice person" and thought "I wonder what his/her books are like?"

So I hope to go and make a pleasant impression, and always go with the intention of meeting new people (and old friends).

It does change between conventions and here size matters. At Comic-Con, the biggest goal is not to get squished in the crowds. At Dragon Con, it's a bit less like that. At Comic-Con, I concentrate more on having a good time than on getting noticed directly because there are so many *huge* names that I'm a very small (and humble) fish in their presence.

At Dragon Con, I have a slightly better presence in the "Anne McCaffrey's Worlds" track and the group there has been coming to Dragon Con mostly since forever. It's a tight-knit group and I'm less worried about being noticed and more interested in having a good time—and helping others to have a good time.

Rob Sawyer

Honestly, at this stage: just to have a good time. See old friends, make new ones, relax. Of course, WorldCon and World Fantasy are mostly about business—meetings with agents, editors, and so on.

Janny Wurts

First priority is to give back to the community, share knowledge and experience and meet new faces. The better this goal is achieved, the happier the attendees and the better the chances they will take the time to see what books or projects I have out. Publicity works best, I've found, when the needs of others are given precedence. Other conventions are done to make ends meet, and if there is a dealer table involved, the first priority, to please others, is split between manning the table and handling direct sales. Some conventions are attended for professional reasons, but those, increasingly, seem to be replaced by other venues.

Mike Resnick

At WorldCon, I line up my work for the following two years, meet new editors, meet foreign editors, learn who's doing unadvertised anthologies, and visit with old friends. At regionals, I just go to enjoy myself and meet friends. If I like the ambiance, I try to return; if I don't like it, it's once and out.

Chelsea Quinn Yarbro

I hope for exposure to more potential readers, and a chance to give a push to my most recent publications. As a side-benefit, it's a chance to get together with friends and colleagues. There is a degree of change that is part of publishing: for example, if Hotel Transylvania wins the special Stoker for The Most Significant Vampire Novel of the (20th) Century this coming weekend, I'd want to push that when discussing the series on any vampire or series-related panel or interview. And mentioning e-reprints is becoming increasingly important as more of the backlist becomes available. Taking the time to participate in a wide variety of appropriate panels and events increases visibility, which is usually worthwhile. The why is because such appearances can get the word out not only effectively but to readers and fans who are not usually in the immediate circle of fans and readers, all of which is beneficial.

Lynn Abbey

What do you hope to accomplish by attending a convention? Does this change between conventions and why? Ideally, I hope to present myself positively to old and new readers. I also hope to have good conversations, often over meals, with people I don't see regularly. The proportion of private v. public activity does change between conventions, but usually not because of the conventions themselves, but because of whatever professional activity I've been up to between the conventions.

Kevin J. Anderson

To raise awareness of a new book, and of me as an author. I hope to get my *Star Wars* or *Dune* readers to read my Seven Suns or Terra Incognita books, for example. I like meeting the fans, meeting fellow writers, meeting booksellers around the country, networking, and I also teach writing workshops, so I enjoy helping new writers. Some cons are primarily working/business trips for me and others are just fun, and some are both.

Kerrie Hughes

Sometimes it's exposure, sometimes it's pleasure, and often it's for the electricity of creativity. I like all three to take place.

John Helfers

Promoting myself as an author, picking up news on possible openings at publishers or editors looking for new projects, and getting the latest publishing news.

Toni Weisskopf

At most conventions I am there to promote the Baen Books line, to meet authors and artists, and for the intellectual stimulation of good panels and good conversations. Sometimes the emphasis changes, depending on who is at the convention.

Melissa Singer

There are three reasons for me to attend conventions. Obviously, I'm there to carry the brand—to act as a representative of my publisher. That's why we do spotlights and talk about the stuff we're publishing in the next few months, why we sometimes throw parties and give things away. We're there to interact with readers as well as writers and agents, and demonstrate that we have good books that people should want to buy and read. The other reason centers on author/agent relations: I might be there to support an author we're already publishing, or to try to make a good impression on someone we're not publishing but want to, or to connect with agents who work in a genre I'm interested in but don't have a lot of contacts in, etc. I also like to share my knowledge and opinions, whether it's about a genre, an author, or the art and craft of writing and publishing.

So what could keep these hard core convention-goers away? Experience has been a hard teacher and it seems that there are things we should all look for.

Todd McCaffrey

Discord, chaos, lack of planning. Any hint of financial impropriety and I'm out of there. Mum was once nearly saddled with the entire costs of a con because the chair was a sleazebag who decided to have a heart attack when the bill came due (and miraculously recovered shortly thereafter).

Rob Sawyer

It's what I don't hear in advance that drives me away. Literally moments before I got your email questions, Bill, I was looking at the websites for several of Canada's annual SF conventions. One hasn't set its date yet. Another hasn't announced its author guest of honour. A third required me to phone the hotel to find out what the convention room rate was. When I see signs of disorganization or lack of planning, I stay away.

Janny Wurts

If a convention has EVER left a professional guest with outstanding bills they had promised to cover, or if there have been troubles with art show theft, or if there are warning flags or known dissent within the community, that definitely puts the damper on.

Mike Resnick

Endless blather about gaming and media guests and programming. There is nothing wrong with either, but they hold no interest for me.

Chelsea Quinn Yarbro

Poor management is off-putting, as is cliquishness among the committee. Also, if the facilities for the convention are awkward or inconvenient.

Lynn Abbey

It's usually not minuses, but pluses that make a difference. If it's a chance to have a reunion with friends, or to meet someone I've admired, or there's something special about the programming or facility, or (especially) if I can combine it with other events/activities.

Kevin J Anderson

In some rare instances, I've heard fellow authors tell horror stories about con staff or how badly a con is run, so that definitely has an influence.

Kerrie Hughes

Not having E-pay to sign up with or a good website in general.

John Helfers

Stories of poor organization and not treating attendees (not just GoHs, but everyday attendees) properly is the biggest reason that makes me to decide to attend or not attend a convention.

Toni Weisskopf

Yes, that's happened. If a convention treats an author badly or is poorly organized.

Melissa Singer

If an editor I work with had an unpleasant time at the same event the previous year, that can make me think twice about attending. Unpleasant: the editor did not make useful connections and/or did not feel that her or his time was utilized well by the convention organizers (we like to work and be helpful); the convention didn't run smoothly/on time.

So Does Size Matter? Should you just go to smaller cons where you will always be noticed? Perhaps big shows with a larger audience will provide more benefits?

Todd McCaffrey

Yes. At the end of the day, attending a convention for a professional is a marketing/public relations operation. You're there to be seen, (hopefully) liked, and to promote your works.

A really small convention may not be worth it. It costs a lot to go to a con and, no matter how much we *all* wish it would be different, very few pros are earning so much money that they can afford to indulge their whims.

So a really small convention is less likely to be attractive than a larger one simply because I can't quite justify the (nearly identical) expense compared to the disparity in potential sales.

On the other hand, some small cons can be very intimate and are worth it just for the other side of con attendance—which I call soul replenishing. Writing is mostly a solitary task and at conventions we authors get a chance to hear that what we're doing makes a difference—and that makes going back to our caves, slitting our veins wide, and pouring our souls out seem worth it.

Rob Sawyer

It actually doesn't. I often enjoy EerieCon in Niagara Falls, New York, and in a good year it gets maybe a hundred warm bodies. I think I mostly prefer cons in the 300- to 500-person range—you get to see the people you want to see; at bigger cons, you miss seeing some people you'd hope to, and that can be very frustrating

Janny Wurts

Size is seldom a factor, because many of the very small conventions tend to appreciate their guests the most!

Mike Resnick

Not to me, no.

Chelsea Quinn Yarbro

Size does matter, and in various ways. Again, one of the nice things about Dragon Con is that since it is huge, I can take occasional short time-outs, which isn't possible in cons of less than 2,500. Also, in a large con, though it demands more "being on" than some, the pay-off in exposure is worth it. Small cons can have many chances to give face-to-face time with fans and readers—which is not always pleasant—and it can provide chances to delve into certain special interest topics in a way that a larger convention cannot reasonably accommodate.

Lynn Abbey

Big conventions (I'm thinking, say, Dragon Con) are spectacles, small conventions are great for meeting new people, and they all have their own personalities.

Kevin J Anderson

My calendar is very full, and I often look forward just to having a few nights in my own bed. Traveling to conventions eats up a lot of writing time, and so I have to weigh the time spent at a con with the time lost on a writing deadline. I enjoy the small, intimate cons and have been to plenty of them, but if I'm going to give up 4-5 writing days, I need to see as many people as possible.

Kerrie Hughes

Yes, when it's too big, handicapped pros/fans find it nearly impossible to attend. It can be anything from wheelchair access to the availability of water and chairs. Often the older professionals are overwhelmed by distances and a lack of help. Some with hidden handicaps, like diabetes or glaucoma, find themselves at a disadvantage because food and signage aren't close or accessible. Too small can be a problem because there isn't enough professional and fan access to make it worthwhile.

John Helfers

Yes, both ways. A large convention has much more chance of attracting the authors/editors you'd like to meet with, but the size can mean that it may be hard to connect with them. A small convention is more intimate, and may lead to more face time with authors and editors, but the smaller attendance limits the networking pool.

Toni Weisskopf

I prefer conventions in the 500-1200 range—big enough to meet new people, small enough to find them. But I also attend both smaller and larger ones.

Melissa Singer

Yes and no. A well-organized large convention can be a more pleasant and worthwhile experience than a poorly-organized small convention. Good programming can make a difference here as well—sometimes a big convention can set up a whole track of programming about the kinds of books I work on, where a small convention might only have one or two panel items that really apply to me. On the other hand, a smaller convention can be entirely focused on areas I work in, whereas some larger conventions can be trying to cover so many areas that they wind up with only one or two things I'm interested in. Whatever the size of the convention, places and ways for people to hang out are important. A small convention where everyone goes to the same bar can be a winner, as can a larger convention with a good Green Room/guest suite.

We asked a couple more authors for recommendations on conventions that they enjoy, and why.

Seanan McGuire won the John W. Campbell award in 2010. She writes fantasy and science fiction novels, filks, cartoons, and has experience in con-running (she ran BayCon for several years). She strongly recommends that if you have never attended a convention, to give it a try. She goes to San Diego Comic-Con every year, and finds it restorative. Authors who attend SDCC and sit in the Authors' Row section of the dealers' hall are mobbed by fans.

Martha Wells is a fantasy and nonfiction author, who has published a dozen well-received fantasy novels. She regularly attends Texas conventions, including AggieCon, ArmadilloCon, ApolloCon and ConDFW. She splurges on one big out-of-state convention per year. Of those she has attended, she likes Norwescon, Boskone and Readercon, for the opportunity to interact with fans. If large crowds overwhelm you, try smaller conventions to start with. If you don't enjoy being at conventions, the fans will see your reaction. There isn't enough of a benefit if you can't bring yourself to relax and have fun. But try. At conventions, you are among your people, those who genuinely understand where you are coming from.

So there you have it, why to go, what to consider, and what to watch out for from the pens of those who have been there (mostly in the bars). What conventions you choose to attend will be a combination of both what you enjoy and what you want to accomplish.

DOING BUSINESS AT A SF CON

ou're there, your publisher is there, so why not? What are the dos and don'ts of working it out at a convention?

Where to Go

Some major conventions are made for business on a large scale. World Fantasy, the Nebulas, and RWA (Romance Writers of America—a growing crossover population with SF authors) have less programming than at many, higher ratio of pros to fans, so they invite opportunity for interaction and networking. Those pros include editors and publishers, as well as a few agents.

Others, like Dragon Con and World Science Fiction Convention, are good large-scale get-togethers with many editors attending and maybe more than a little business. They often provide a great opportunity to interact with other authors you had not met before. You may be a face in the crowd, but you have the chance to meet other writers who work for your publisher, not to mention other members of the editorial staff who wouldn't bother with or aren't needed at a smaller event. You could even end up sitting in on a wide-ranging business chat among fellow professionals that could work out very advantageously for you.

Smaller conventions may not be of much use to you, businesswise, unless your editor (or the editor you wish to make yours) is attending. If s/he is, it might be worthwhile for you to go, if only to make that connection. They have the advantage of you not getting lost in the crowd and the chance for some serious face time if things click.

Schmoozing for work

Any convention with a large concentration of editors and fellow authors presents the possibility of finding paying work. Face to face, you can ask an editor what it is s/he is looking for. If that sparks an idea, mention it, and ask if you can submit it. If you're in a panel and hear editors discussing the tragic lack of a desired subject crossing their desks, and you just happen to have such a manuscript on your hard drive, approach one of them later on and make your pitch.

If you're a short-story writer, take the time to get to know the most prolific anthologists. The staff of Tekno Books used to be the clearing house for dozens of anthologies a year. Since the sad passing of Martin H. Greenberg, Tekno remains, but the short story market has fragmented. E-publishers, small presses, small e-presses, magazines and direct electronic publishing opportunities such as Amazon, Smashwords and others have become the more frequent repositories for shorter fiction. It's far easier to learn about upcoming anthologies in whatever format by talking to fellow authors and editors at a convention. By the time you read about an anthology it, and probably further volumes, have been delivered.

Mike Resnick, multiple Hugo Award winner and relentless networker, considers WorldCon his favorite hunting ground:

"For more than a third of a century I've been lining up most of the following two years' work at WorldCon. There is simply no better venue for meeting/schmoozing domestic and foreign editors and publishers, finding out who's editing the unadvertised invite-only anthologies, presenting yourself to new publishers, getting market info from your peers, etc. It's a day-in day-out thing, it doesn't end with WorldCon, but you accomplish more at WorldCon (or at least I do) than in the rest of the year combined."

Act in a professional manner

I know we keep pounding that lesson home, but in every generation of new authors, there's at least one who hasn't been sufficiently socialized to have absorbed it. Even if you are awkward or shy, being polite, grateful, prompt and responsible will cover up most sins. Apologize if you overstep. You can do more damage to your reputation than your skill with words can repair by being a surly boor one time at one convention. If you are a new writer, that can derail your career. John Helfers, formerly of Tekno Book, edited for Stonehenge Press , and now is busy as a freelance editor, mentions what he calls the Four P's: politeness, professionalism, patience and persistence.

Remember people's names! Con-coms are notorious for printing the name of the convention in humongous letters on the badge, but dropping down to ten-point type for names. If you don't hear a name well over the hubbub in the dealers' room or a room party, ask again. It's not rude to want to get the editor's name right. Spelling can count too. Or the sales director, or the art director, or (*God-forbid-don't-ever-antagonize*) the assistant or office manager. If you're bad at names, repeat it a few times to yourself and write it down the first chance you get. Ask for their business cards. Write the date and the convention name on the back. (You'll be glad later that you did.) Offer your own card. Have a stack with you.

The Hows, Wheres, and Wherefores

If you know that an editor or agent you want to meet is going to the convention, it might be best to try and arrange a meeting in advance. Your schedule will fill up, and so will your editor's. As soon as you have received your program schedule (meaning your editor now—probably—has hers), get in touch, preferably by e-mail, and ask to set up a date. State the openings in your schedule. Offer to buy coffee, lunch, dinner, a drink, whatever your budget will allow. (It is also acceptable to ask to meet in the Green Room, though that has its own pitfalls, as we'll discuss below.) Know something about the person and company you are approaching, but not in the way of a stalker contemplating a victim. You're looking for a job—how do you fit into their needs? As John Helfers puts it, "Few things are more damaging than not being aware of the various genres that editor or agent handles—especially if your book is diametrically opposite of what they sell or publish!"

If you can't arrange a meeting in advance, your option is to approach the person at the convention, as early as possible. Naturally, you want to get down to business right away, but that is not the best approach. Be courteous and deferential, of course, but make the connection. Express your interest in a non-threatening, friendly way, briefly and to the point. Find a neutral meeting point, such as a publisher's party (not theirs, at which they will likely be hosting and have no time for a business conversation). Ask if s/he has time to sit down with you—say, in the bar—and hear what you have to say. This is one of the greatest things about writing SF and fantasy: access to the publishers. Romance writers in particular often say that their relationship with their Romance editors is much more formal than with the editors they write for at SF houses.

We can't put it better than Melissa Singer of TOR Books:

"There are plenty of old stories about how not to approach an editor—and it's my hope that most people know the basic rules, but in just case, here are a few:

"Don't follow me into the bathroom (this has actually happened to me a few times). If I'm going to the bathroom, it's either because I really need to use it (because I've just been on a panel for an hour) or because I need a few minutes away from the convention floor and don't want to go back to my room. I don't know how many editors feel this way, but most of the time when I'm at a convention, I'm "on," and once in a while I need to chill out, just for a minute or two. Bathrooms are good places for that but not if people want to have conversations while I'm hiding.

"Pay attention to an editor's body language. After a panel, if we're not being thrown out of the room right away, it's perfectly okay to come up to the front and ask for a business card or try to arrange to meet at another time for a pitch. If, however, the editor is standing up and packing her bag or edging toward the door, that means that the editor has somewhere else to be. This means that it's not a good time to talk, even just to arrange to meet later. Because if there are a bunch of people who all want to have those same few words with an editor, then the editor will be late for whatever the next thing is. Sometimes editors will remember to say, at the beginning of the panel, that they have to rush away at the end, but usually they don't. We are sorry when we have to rush, but depending on the convention or conference, we may be participating in several panels or workshops … or we may want to actually go and listen to another panel or workshop, especially if we are working with someone appearing there. Editors generally work in genres that they are interested in; even at a convention/conference where we are there to spend time with writers, we often want to see/hear some of the convention/conference because the topics interest us. The corollary to this is that if I'm sitting in on a panel or workshop, please don't pitch to me. For one thing, it's rude when there's conversation in the audience and, for another, I probably want to listen to the speakers."

Editors come to conventions knowing that writers will want to talk to them, and most make themselves available as much as they can. "When I represented the various Five Star lines for Tekno Books and attended a convention," John Helfers told us, "I was pretty much available every time I stepped out of my hotel room. Since I was there as a draw for authors, I felt it was important to make myself as reachable as possible for whomever wanted to meet or talk to me."

Since editors and agents are much in demand at a convention, to have time to get to know one, you might have to share your face time. Melissa Singer likes the camaraderie of a group meal.

"Editors are human too. While we are at a conference/convention for work and to be available to writers and agents, it's nice to have some conversations that aren't pitches. If we're talking about TV or movies or books or school or raising children or our pets or whatever, one on one with you or in a group, don't abruptly start to pitch. Most editors will ask you, at some point in the conversation, if you write, what you're working on, etc. We know that this subtext lies under most conversations when we're meeting people for the first time and we won't leave you hanging, but we like the fantasy that you might like us as a person (just as we want to like you as a person).

"If it's a small convention/conference, we might even have mealtimes free. At RWA events, I frequently wind up tagging along with a group of writers for dinner—people I met that afternoon or at the panel right before the dinner break. I like to hang out over food. Others prefer to hang out in the bar (I do that too, but I don't drink alcohol much when I'm working, and bars are often a little too noisy for me; despite being from a big, noisy city, I am really sensitive to noise).

"All that said—and I like meeting writers and hanging out with them at conventions—I think there are only a handful of times that meeting someone for the first time at a convention has led fairly directly to a deal. Indirectly that happens plenty, of course, but it's just one element in my decision-making. The work itself still comes first, for me."

In other words, don't dismiss the benefit of a purely social interaction. You may not have what they want at one convention, but having broken the ice, you should find it easier to approach them again later, when you do have the right proposal in hand. A shared meal or a publisher's room party will also give you the opportunity to get to know your fellow writers who work for that house. More than one collaboration has resulted from matchmaking by editors (and fellow writers) on seeing chemistry between authors.

The Green Room, the con suite/panel preparation area/chill-out zone for the attending professionals, is a useful spot to sit down with an editor or agent. The members-only nature of the room keeps you from being interrupted by fans, so you have some privacy to make your pitch. On the other hand, your conversation may be frequently interrupted by other authors who want a piece of your guest's time. Be patient. The editor has not forgotten your presence. That said, don't waste the time you have.

Not generally advised: trying to make a pitch at a publisher's room party. Sometimes the editors talk business with certain authors at their party, but often they are busy being hosts and don't want to be pulled away from the majority of their guests. You might make a polite query as to whether s/he has time to listen to a brief pitch, but be prepared to take no for an answer.

Pitch Sessions

Pitch sessions are far less common at SF/Fantasy conventions than they are at romance conventions, but they are not unknown. John Helfers recommends coming prepared with a thirty-second version of your plot, expandable to perhaps two to four minutes that goes into further detail, and be ready to answer questions. He adds, "it's all right to be a bit nervous, so be sure to practice your pitch until you're comfortable with it, and if your mind does happen to go blank while talking to someone, take a moment, take a deep breath, and go back to the last point you remember making, and continue with what you're saying."

At romance conventions, Melissa Singer usually participates in a few hours' worth of pitch sessions. "If you're at a conference like that and you want to pitch to me, please sign up! People are sometimes reluctant to sign up; most of the time I have appointments available. But make sure that what you pitch is something I—or my publisher—will be interested in. Look at what we publish before you pitch; go to the 'what we're looking for' panel if it takes place before your pitch session. Remember that 99% of the time, editors will not take submissions from you at the convention. Even on a flash drive. Even a query letter. Even a sheet listing all the novels you are working on (by the way, this is a particularly bad idea; while I want to know that you have more than one idea, presenting me with a list of 30—none finished—does not impress me. I want to know that you have the diligence and focus to finish a book or two, not begin a dozen different ones). Have a business card—one with some white space on it is always nice; I like to jot down the title and genre of something that I ask to see, so that I can remember it, and you, when it comes in.

"At SF/F conventions, if there are no pitch sessions scheduled, it is perfectly okay to ask if you can pitch. If I'm not busy, I'll hear you out right then. If I am, I'll suggest another time/place."

In other words, be prepared to talk about something that you have finished and can send immediately to the editor if s/he likes what you have discussed.

Toni Weisskopf, publisher of Baen Books, prefers to use conventions for their social interaction. "For me, cons are a chance to get to meet authors I might not see otherwise. I've met most of the authors I work with for the first time at a con, in fact. That said, for *new* authors who are trying to sell me something, it's not ideal. I buy stories, not plot synopses or charming anecdotes, so while going to a convention to check out the panels and learn about the industry is a good strategy for a new author, going solely to buttonhole an editor to sell your story is not, at least from my point of view. I'm always happy to talk to folks, if I'm not running from panel to appointment, etc., but my reaction will always boil down to: I can't tell if I like it until I read it, so please just follow our regular submission guidelines."

Advised: chat with a receptive editor about proposed plotlines (knowing you will have to send him or her a reminder of your discussion along with your manuscript—what is discussed at a con is frequently forgotten by the time your editor has reached the jet to go home). Ask if they have something they would like to see from you. As with the edit of your finished manuscript, your proposals have an interactive element. Get editors' input when you can see their reactions. The editor who buys your first book is a significant person in your career.

Even a casual discussion may result in a sale. Jack McDevitt sat down with his editor at lunch, and was pleasantly surprised at the outcome. "Three years after having published my first novel, I was still uncertain where I stood and wondered how receptive my editor would be to an idea I had been thinking about. Or, for that matter, to a second novel at all. When I broached the subject over a lunch, asking whether she'd be interested in seeing a proposal, she pushed a napkin in my direction and told me to write the proposal."

Not advised: *pushing* for a quick decision at a con. There are so many factors involved in whether the book you want to write is a good match for your chosen house. Keep it friendly. Pushing for an answer may make that answer "no" when it might have been otherwise after giving them time to consider.

Even more unadvised: Helfers states it clearly: "When an author gives the impression that they are doing you a favor by talking to you, or when they haven't done their homework on the publishing house, and think that I can somehow make an exception to our rules for them."

Should you turn in manuscripts at conventions? Not unless your publisher drove. And specifically asked you to give the manuscript to him or her there. What with the current punitive fees for luggage (apparently about to get even worse for Spirit Airline passengers), no one wants to add several pounds of paper to his or her bags, especially when UPS or Federal Express can convey it directly to the publishing house with no sore back or hard feelings.

Shopping for an Agent

For some writers, getting an agent may be more important than finding a publishing house. After all, if you have an agent, you can put your business into their hands and get back to the job of writing, while s/he does the job of selling what you write. As we mentioned above, in SF/Fantasy we can make connections directly with editors, but to branch out into more genres, or cross-genres, it's useful to have an agent.

As anyone who has tried to get one can attest, agents are hard to come by. They can only handle so many clients at a time. If they have openings in their client list, a brief meeting might give you an edge over another writer who has only written them a letter. Even better, a convention will let an agent see you in action. John Betancourt met his first agent, Don Maass, at a convention.

"He took me out to lunch after hearing me speak on a panel, and almost before I knew it, we were in business ...

and he went on to sell a dozen or so books for me. Nothing beats a personal contact, especially with an editor or an agent ... assuming you make a good impression!"

Ethan Ellenberg of the Ethan Ellenberg Agency, offers cautiously optimistic advice.

"You learn a lot about someone face to face. It's far more possible to have a wide ranging, spontaneous discussion at a convention. So, I recommend it. One caveat, before actually signing anything or with anyone, do go home and think about it and a do a full 'due diligence.' My good experiences at conventions have always been learning of an exciting new project that an author might have held off on discussing. Conventions are worthwhile and doing business in person is worthwhile, but don't get carried away by the moment."

Working at a Con

This is as opposed to asking for work. Most writers often do this. Deadlines wait for no convention. Your laptop can travel with you. Jody tends to use hers as a mobile manuscript repository for readings and to send stories she discussed with fellow writers to them. In other words, our laptops are extensions of ourselves—the external memory banks that are easier to read and work on than your phone. The implanted device surely can't be too far in the future. (Moore's Law, call your office.)

As for writing at a con, that is down to your powers of concentration and your ability to compartmentalize usefully. Unless you're a total exhibitionist who likes to write, say, in a storefront window, no one but you and your roommates should know you're working. Perhaps that is the way you set yourself apart from other writers, by proving you can work anywhere, but to the rest of us it comes across as pretentious, even obnoxious.

Don't let writing distract you from why you are there, or why did you spend the money to go? Some writers find the change of scenery refreshing and can get a lot done in between panels and parties. If you must write, due to deadlines, inspiration or natural crankiness if you don't crank out words daily (you know who you are), do not let it interfere with the events in which you have promised to participate for the convention. There are few phrases more egotistical than, "I forgot about the panel because I was writing." Adding insult to injury would be to infer that what you were writing was far more interesting than anything you could have been discussing on the panel. Word *will* spread. (See the previous article on being a good convention guest.) Know that the Internet is forever, and depending on what social media are in operation, there could be anything from a tweet to a YouTube video demonstrating what a jerk you are.

Some of the down sides:

Unless you're famous for living a pirate lifestyle or you have written a book on Japanese kimonos, you are a leading costumer, or you belong to the ethnicity whose costume you are wearing, it's inadvisable to wear costumes while being a pro. Utilikilts don't count. (They're, well, pants.) Neither do Regency costumes at a Regency ball. Costume-wearers tend not to be taken as seriously as authors in civilian dress. Our words should speak for themselves. Few actors attend conventions dressed as their characters. It's a shame, because many of us have a closetful of costumes and would love to play dress-up. It has become more important to us to use the convention as a professional appearance.

You can't do everything. It's entirely possible that your responsibilities to the convention will take up all your available time, leaving you with no opportunity to meet with that editor. Steal a moment to hand them a business card. That is worthwhile, if not as satisfying as taking a meeting. You've made the connection. If they're interested in you, perhaps they will come to one of your panels. Impress them, and you've accomplished an important part of your purpose. Maybe at your next convention you can sit down with them one on one.

SMALL CONVENTIONS

All conventions started small. Even the first WorldCon in 1939 had at most only two hundred attendees. You may scoff at a small convention as a professional venue, but a budding writer will never have a better chance to go one-on-one and sell him/herself to readers and potential readers. (That said, for the beginning pro, a small con might not be the very best first convention.) It is a good way to hone your publicity chops, and offers opportunities that larger conventions may not.

Where to find them

Even in a city that hosts larger, well-established science fiction conventions, smaller events can be found. For example, Chicago has three annual fan-based regionals, Windycon (November), Capricon (February), and Duckon (June), as well as Chicago Comic-Con (July), but it also has had a plethora of smaller events, such as G-FEST, OpCon,

CODCON, Evanston Writers Workshop Conference, and MuseCon.

Locating them can be a challenge unless their volunteers have thoughtfully left flyers on the freebie tables of larger events, because small cons have limited resources in terms of staff and money. As with boutique publishers, the Internet has given boutique conventions an easier way to reach potential attendees. You may see a mention of a new event forwarded to you on Twitter or Facebook. Most of the time, though, you are likely to hear of them through word of mouth. ("Hey, we're holding a con in April!")

We have to distinguish here between small conventions, consisting of 100 to 500 attendees, and *really* small ones. The latter can be a lot of fun, but tend to have a focused theme, such as Star Trek, furries, anime, comics, relax-a-con, zines, British SF, Aaron Sorkin*, etc. Depending upon your personal interests and profile, they might be worth going to as attendees, but not necessarily in a professional capacity. Unless you have an infinity of free weekends, you might want to consider the former instead.

One of the most common venues for small conventions is colleges, as well as the occasional forward-thinking high school. If there is an active SF society on campus, chances are that an event has at least been under discussion, if not ventured and held. Two of the cons listed in the first paragraph above are school-based: OpCon (Oak Park-River Forest High School), and CODCON (College of Dupage County, IL). StellarCon, in High Point, NC, is sponsored by the University of North Carolina Greensboro. I-CON (which has long ago outgrown the small convention designation) hails from SUNY Stony Brook, NY. Most recently, we attended ConJour in Houston, held at the University of Houston—Clear Lake. Check you local junior colleges and private colleges as well as state schools. Many have SF conventions attached, almost all have clubs or groups of some sort.

Many other small conventions are offshoots of a larger regional. There you will find more experienced con-runners as well as knowledgeable fans.

Why Go?

As with any convention, you are there to meet people and get the word out about your work. A small event may seem less worthy than a major event, but a cozy venue makes a great setting for a few select pros.

What's in it for you?

Unlike larger conventions, a free membership is not always a given, unless you are asked to be the guest of honor (and maybe not even then, depending on budget; Many years ago Jody's first guest of honor convention asked her to pay $5.00 toward her membership). However, budgets vary greatly. A small con may not be an impecunious one. They might have the money for airfare, hotel and meals for one or more guests.

Feeling out the financial situation is as delicate a matter as asking someone their salary. What you may hope for depends on who asked whom. If a con approaches you, tell them your needs and negotiate. If they cannot afford to fly you in, for example, but can offer money for gas (no small expense these days), decide what you can live with. They may not give you a per diem for food but have someone cooking three meals a day for the con suite or Green Room, as ConJour in Houston does (and excellent baked goods!). You may get a t-shirt and/or tote bag, whatever they can afford.

If you approach the convention, however, you are largely volunteering your services. It's good for your karma, if not your pocketbook.

What you can expect out of the arrangement is a chance to shine, to be a big, or medium-sized, frog in a small pond. The fan base that attends small events is dedicated to science fiction and fantasy books and media. You will get a lot of face time with a motivated audience. While everything you do will receive more scrutiny than it would if you were one of myriad guests, you will be appreciated all the more.

A small event may also be your best shot at your first guest of honor slot. If you make your interest known, they may put you on the roster for the upcoming year.

What is expected of you

The primary tools you need to employ are flexibility and patience. Almost every convention committee is made up of unpaid volunteers. We have said this in previous articles, but it bears emphasizing with regard to a small event. The people running the con are not professionals. It may be that none of them has ever managed anything larger than a birthday party. Bring your low blood pressure along and cut them considerable slack. Many elements that you expect from larger, long-time conventions will fall through the cracks. You may be scheduled on back-to-back-to-back-to-back panels. They may forget to pay for your room (do NOT pay for it yourself and expect to be reimbursed later; many are the horror stories that we have heard from pros who found their credit cards charged by the hotel because something went wrong with the convention's finances). They may forget about your food allergies, time constraints, health problems—but none of this is out of malice. Let your con-com know if there are any non-negotiables. If you are allergic to peanuts, insulin-dependent, night-blind, or anything that will seriously impair your ability to perform or endanger your life, they need to know that. Remind them—gently—and they will do their best for you. You may not see your schedule until moments before your first panel (or shortly after ...). You may not GET a copy of your schedule. Stuff happens. Please do your best to make do with the least that you need to perform.

If you are easy-going and let minor annoyances pass, everyone will have a good time, including you. (You are permitted by law, however, to drag into your hotel room and strangle anyone who staggers drunkenly past your door at four AM shrieking and banging on walls.)

This is the time to trot out any additional talents you have. Do you filk? Show up at the filk singing. Can you tell stories to young fen? Do you know anything about costumes? Will you help judge the costume contest? You can have enormous fun at the judges' table at many small conventions. Just because there are only a few contestants doesn't mean some of them aren't gems. Can you auctioneer? Many authors have banged the gavel at numerous events. Both get you in front a large crowd in a positive way. Be a good audience member at other panels than the ones to which you are assigned. The membership will be thrilled that you have jumped in to participate.

Face it, you are going to be a major portion of the entertainment, so be prepared to spend most of your time "on." Because you are one of the few pros present, you will be scheduled for every panel they can squeeze you onto. You may be assigned a kaffeeklatsch or "an hour with" interview. If you are guest of honor, you are expected to make a speech at opening ceremonies, and, provided you are still there, offer thanks at closing ceremonies/dead dog party. The convention committee may want a little private time with you, such as coffee or a dinner.

A small convention is also a great place to hang out with the other professionals present. Because there are so few of you, you'll be thrown frequently into one another's company. It's a terrific opportunity to get to know fellow pros and have fun with them.

If you are gracious and helpful, you will almost certainly be invited back. If you wish to be. It is no bad thing to become part of the stable of a friendly small convention. It makes a nice change from the hustle-bustle of the big events.

*Sorry. Irresistible in-joke from an article by *The Onion* satirical newspaper, which published a "review" of "Sor-Kon," a convention dedicated to fans of *The West Wing* and other Aaron Sorkin productions. It was so convincing that a writer I know was trying to find out how to go to the next one before s/he realized where the article had been published.

Panel Self-Defense

Jerkus egotisticus, *n.*, unfortunately extremely prevalent in panel environments, and possessed of a kind of prosopagnosia (face blindness) because they cannot recognize themselves, either in mirrors or in pointed remarks.

In the thirty-some years we've been on convention panels, there have been times when the mood behind the table is less than collegial. Considering that we are there to be entertainment and education for the audience, it's dismaying when one's fellow panelists forget exactly why they're there and what they are supposed to do. When the program director assembles a group to discuss a certain topic, the tacit understanding is that each person is chosen because of her/his expertise, point of view and eloquence on the subject. Unfortunately, we've experienced so many ways that the perfect expression of those opinions is prevented from reaching that audience. Here are some of the means of interference, with suggestions on combatting them.

The Clique:

If you are new to an area of the country, or just new to a certain convention, especially a long-running one, chances are you are going to run into people who have known one another for many years, who have fallen into a pattern on panels that they have done every year since the con began. They know who's going to talk about what, who disagrees with whom, and to whom they defer within that small group. Seeing a stranger sitting at the table will most often prompt introductions and expressions of welcome. Sometimes it won't. You may receive a cold stare that asks wordlessly, "What are YOU doing here?" The best thing to do is, without rancor, introduce yourself and give your 25-word précis on why you're on the panel. If you have the time, make a point of exchanging a few words with the moderator. S/he is your ally, or ought to be (see the chapter on moderating panels, too), and will make sure you get a chance to talk.

As an unknown factor, the rest of the panel could respond to your presence in a number of ways. They might try to make an ally of you. They might embrace you, or try to ignore you. This is where your connection to the moderator is important.

One of the main reasons you are on a panel is to make a connection with the audience and give people a reason to look for your books afterward. That's why your fellow pros are there, too. Everyone wants as much attention as they can get. Respond to the topics raised by the moderator as coherently and briefly as you can. You don't have to be neutral, if you vehemently disagree with what is being said, but be cordial. Since you were put on the same panel, you have something important to contribute to the topic. If all goes well, you might make a connection or two before the hour ends. Be open to it. A really good panel is one in which you have a good time and collect a few business cards and contact info as well.

Sectarianism:

Because you're an unknown, the others won't know whether you agree with their agenda. Just because SF is the literature of ideas and the future doesn't mean it has fundamentally changed the personalities of human beings. Old acquaintances will pass plenty of remarks among themselves. They were still born in the decades they were born in, and may make remarks to which you rightly object. But do not lump everyone of a seeming demographic together. Plenty of feminists live in our small society, and not all of them are female, and not all of them are young. Plenty of friends of LGBT lifestyle are not members of those groups. Plenty of stoic defenders exist of those who were not born with their characteristics or backgrounds. Don't assume, based upon a scan of the table, that you're among enemies. There is a maxim, coined by noted cinematographer Jack Hofstra: "Assumption is the mother of all fuckups." Keep it in mind, and maintain an open outlook.

SF writers and fans are more open-minded than almost any other group out there. Ignorance is not aggression. Don't forget the second function of a panel: to educate. Teach them something they don't know. Believe that they are there to learn.

You may have audience members who do indeed have a negative agenda. If a fellow panel member is under attack, do speak up. If you are under attack, defend yourself, but it is only appropriate to attack the argument, not the person. The moderator should also step in to defuse the situation and possibly eject the troublemakers.

Spotlight:

There will be panels in which the audience is there to see only one participant. All the questions will be directed to that person. The moderator might even fawn on that person, neglecting everyone else. Really, in this case, there's nothing you can do to change the situation. If you happen to be a fan of the One Panelist, take the opportunity to fanboy/girl/being a little. Make the most of your opportunity. Ask them the questions you've always wanted to. Frankly, that will put the audience on your side. They're there for the One Panelist, and appreciate others who share their passion.

If you're not, if to you the One Panelist is just another writer, we advise you to live with it. It's one hour of your life. No experience is wasted. Take notes. Put the situation into one of your stories. If you grouse about it aloud or in public, you'll be seen as small and petty. It's not worth the momentary satisfaction.

If you happen to be the spotlighted guest, imagine how you would feel if you were one of the less-lighted panelists. Chances are you can't open up the attention of the audience to your fellows, but be gracious. If anyone is openly resentful of your position, accept that as part of the cost of fame.

Me, Me, Me!

There are panels in which one person will take over, exhibiting some kind of bad behavior. Over the years, those have included the panelist complaining that the time is one s/he considers uncivilized, so the panelist deems him- or herself above social niceties; refusing to engage with either one's fellow panelists and/or the audience in a form of personal agenda; grumbling over some petty facet of the topic; spouting non-sequiturs; or not speaking at all. That's on them, not on you.

Just because someone has the expertise or fame to be in demand on panels does not mean they have the social graces to handle the exposure. They may insult their fellow panelists, cause all manner of disruption such as overwhelming them when they try to speak, verbal abuse, up to and even including physical attack (we have alluded elsewhere to the science panelist who assaulted a fellow speaker, who happened to be in a wheelchair).

It will serve you best to hold to the topic. We don't say that will be easy. Jody has a particular memory of a World Fantasy event in which seven other members were held hostage by a reasonably well-known person who did not like the topic under discussion and refused to talk about it. He hijacked the panel. Admittedly, the rest of the participants were trying to defer to him, and were too polite to call him out. Therefore, the panel was a farce. The moderator could do nothing. It was, thankfully, soon over. (nb.: this will never happen again.—JLN) This capitulation does not serve the convention or the audience.

Again, in this case, the moderator should set the tone and try to shepherd the boor along with the rest of you. It may not be possible to run the panel smoothly, but please do not be that person. Don't be another problem for the moderator. If the bad behavior is more than you can take, you can leave, but in this case, departing will draw more attention to you than to the irritant. If you're not being attacked directly, we implore you to stick it out.

Ad hominem (attacks on you, not on your arguments)

Personal offense is another matter entirely. If someone, either on the panel or in the audience, attacks you directly, call them on it. A facial expression of deep shock and horror is appropriate for these moments. The other panelists, even the audience, may chime in at this point, but it is up to the moderator to control the situation. S/he should call a halt to personal attacks at once. Try not to engage with the attacker. Do not feed the trolls. It's not worth it

Never launch *ad hominem* attacks yourself. You can't win, either in the argument or the court of public opinion. Appearance-shaming is particularly egregious, because people can't help their looks. The comedian Jay Leno always says when he makes fun of someone, it's based upon their choices. If a bald man is sitting in the front row, he'll make fun of his tie instead of his head. Divert, defuse, and get back to the topic.

You always have the right to ask for help if someone is picking on you. If there is no help, you can walk out. No panel is so important that you need to put up with open attacks. If the abuser follows you, go directly to program ops or the nearest con-com member with a walkie-talkie, a security guard, or a police officer. In any case, do not let yourself be alone with that person.

If you suspect that you may be scheduled at a convention alongside someone who has a habit of abusing you ad hominem, use the program participant application to name those with who you do not wish to appear on panels. It is almost always kept confidential. If enough people decline to appear with your problem child, it is more likely than not that the con-com will schedule the rest of you, and not the irritant. I've heard complaints from some would-be program participants that they have very few items on their schedules. See the dictionary definition above.

Intimidation

Like many ills in society, it's hard to say whether intimidation is becoming more widespread on panels or more widely reported. We have talked with program participants, largely female, many of them new to the field, who say that they have not been allowed to talk on panels, or have been overridden, drowned out, or ignored by the other panelists and even the moderator. If this has happened to you, first please apply the "reasonable person" assessment: if you had been a man, a professor, a movie star, a republican, cute, thin, a gay rights activist, or whatever the makeup of the panel had been, would this still have happened to you? If the answer is no, you have grounds for a complaint.

Take control, as much as you are able. If you can, show that you find the bad behavior comical rather than threatening. You can be funny and still get your point across. If a group of panelists is hogging the one functional mike at the end of the table and snarling or blanking anyone who reaches for it or tries to make their own point, go over and take it away from them. Then, speak your piece. Then, pointedly hand it to someone else who was disenfranchised by the obnoxious set. The audience will laugh. You may even start some byplay over the disputed mike. And you may never get it back again in that hour. But you will have made a mark, for yourself and those who will have to share the stage next time with the boors.

If you're too shy to respond in an outward or outrageous fashion, you will need to tolerate it, at least for that hour. Take the moral high ground. Remember it and report it.

In summary, it's all down to you

No one will give you respect you do not demand for yourself, and by that we do not mean shrill complaints. Everyone will remember what behavior you display in public; if you act out in a fashion detrimental to your reputation, someone will remember it and repeat it. Everything is reflected today on the Internet. It's more than possible that panel discussions or workshops will be recorded, either by the convention committee for later distribution or sale, or by an audience member. You don't know when you will end up on YouTube. Make sure that your public face is professional and cool.

Make use of the program participant survey. If you have had bad experiences in the past with certain pros, tell the convention ahead of time you do not want to be on panels with them. They will respect your wishes. Yes, it may cut down on the number of events that include you, but you won't have to fight for the mike with a *Jerkus egotisticus*. Chances are, as we have said, *Jerkus egotisticus* may find himself without events instead. If there is no survey, contact the con-com directly and ask what to do. Don't name the aggressor until you are asked. E-mails are too easily copied and forwarded.

Appeal to the moderator. There are overwhelming personalities in our field. Some of them will take control where they see an opening. A good moderator might be able to jolly them back into line. Few con-runners will assign one of those overwhelming writers to be the moderator, knowing that a panel will turn into a monologue. A strong moderator won't let the panel get out of hand or off topic.

Report the problem to your affinity group. SFWA has a grievance committee. In all likelihood, so do HWA, Sisters in Crime, RWA and Authors Guild. Make use of it. If several panelists have been intimidated or abused at a particular convention, it may have a toxic corporate culture. Most con-coms are truly interested in their guests having a good time. A few are insular little fiefdoms. Share your concerns so others won't go through what you did.

Protect yourself. If you honestly fear for your safety, either during or after a panel, walk with someone, even if you have to conscript another panelist or an audience member as a companion. Report the problem to the concom. Take refuge in ops or the Green Room or the hotel office where you have witnesses. Scream if you have to. Call the police if you must. Tell others that you are having a problem with So-and-so. (You may find you're not alone in So-and-so picking on you.)

Practice. If you're shy, role-play with a few friends on how to handle difficult panelists. Like any other form of self-defense, if you create a mental "muscle memory," you'll have an automatic tool or two to which your mind will snap over if any of the situations above come up.

There is a major difference between being a good writer and being a good panelist. A panelist is at conventions to entertain. Welcome to show biz! Some excellent and compelling writers are terrible panelists. They express themselves incredibly well on paper and on the Internet, and not at all in person. You may have a lot to say, but can you say it aloud, pithily, and in an entertaining fashion? If not, perhaps being on panels is not for you yet. When you feel more confident, go for it. We're waiting to hear your voice.

Practical Tips for Moderating a Panel

Fairly soon after you begin attending conventions as a pro, you may find yourself being asked to be the moderator of a panel. You will be expected to guide and lead a public discussion by a group of your fellow pros and other attendees selected because of their interest in or expertise on a certain topic. This can be relatively challenging, but is a great showcase for you as a person and an author. Moderating also helps to put you in front of and establish rapport with the better known authors on the panel. Later, having been the moderator of a stimulating discussion gives you common ground later to chat about with them. Here are a few hints and suggested techniques you can use when moderating that will help you to maintain control and ensure that the panel is the most fun for both those watching and participating in it.

1. Always start a panel with introductions. You do not introduce everyone in a traditional manner. Just start

on one end and ask each panelist to state who they are and why they are on that particular panel. This gives you not only the names of those you do not know (and especially their pronunciation), but also some idea of what aspects of the panel's topic each one can speak best on. Make note of this information to ask questions later that you are assured they will have an answer to or opinion on. First names are generally appropriate for you to use when calling on a panelist. Exceptions to this are those with titles related to the topic (Doctor Smith), office holders (Councilman Brown), and clerics (Sister Mary Jones), or if the panelists introduce themselves using a title and no first name.

2. Keep in mind your job on the panel changes when you go from panelist to moderator. As a panelist, the panel is an opportunity for you to impress the audience, by entertaining or informing them, so they will go out and buy your books. Now, your goal is to draw out from the rest of the panel's great answers, stories, and examples. That is not to say you cannot interject your own observations, but do not use your authority to dominate the discussions. You will look better and attract more readers maintaining an exciting discussion than you will by trying to put yourself forward. Prepare a list of questions in advance. If you know who your fellow panelists will be, write some with them in mind. Write more questions than you think you will need. Being prepared will help prevent embarrassing gaps in the

discussion or allowing someone else to take over the discussion. You are there to lead it. Then don't let your list dominate the discussion. If it moves in a direction you did not expect, but is interesting, feel free to discard your list of questions and wing it.

3. If you see another author in the audience who is not on the panel but is a known expert on the topic being discussed, it is okay to ask them to join the panel before it starts. But if you plan to do this, be sure to very quietly ask the scheduled panelists if any of them object. If even one does, it's probably best not to ask the new author to participate. There may be a reason that author has not been assigned that panel. Do not add anyone once the panel has started.

4. When you begin as moderator, welcome everyone for coming. If there are children in the audience, mention that the panel will try to keep its language appropriate. By doing that, you put the panelists on notice in a positive way and avoid later problems. (It's embarrassing for everyone to have a parent shepherd a child out because the discussion became too adult.) If it is likely that phrases or ideas covered may be upsetting to some, a verbal warning at the start to whomever has young fans there so they can leave will avoid awkwardness or even hurt later.

5. It is okay to begin the first few rounds of a discussion on a panel by having each panelist in turn answer until everyone has spoken. This works very well if the question is defining what the panel is about. ("To begin, why don't each of us tell us what avian fantasy

is. Let's start at the left side.") This breaks the ice and gets them all talking. Soon you may find that those who have something to say will jump in, and the discussion will become less structured. As the moderator, whether you answer each of these early questions you set is optional.

6. Make sure each panelist gets a say several times during the panel. You do not need to make certain each panelist answers every question or topic, but rather give them a chance to speak when they have something to contribute. If a panelist has been quiet for a long time, try asking them to analyze what was just said from their perspective as an (editor, new author, athlete, bricklayer or whatever distinguishes them on the panel). Try to find something the quiet panelist will be confident saying.

7. Don't demand that a panelist talks about something out of their realm of experience. This is embarrassing for all involved and makes you both look bad. You are a moderator, not a dictator. It is not necessary that every panelist have a comment or opinion on each topic.

8. If panelists want to jump in following the comments of another pro, let them. Even if they drift a bit off topic, this is not a problem. After a few comments, ask a new question to bring things back in line. Do not try to always steer the conversation or its direction. You are not there to guarantee the topic is fully covered. You are there to ensure those listening and those speaking are entertained and informed.

Some of the greatest panels have been because they went off topic. Where they drifted was more interesting and exciting than the narrow description in the schedule. It's better to be informative, entertaining, and most of the time just on something vaguely related than rigidly adhering to the original topic.

9. If one speaker is talking too much, the best way to interrupt them is to jump in and agree at the end of their next sentence with something they just said, then ask for the opinion of another panelist about the talkative person's answer. This allows you to regain control of the flow while making the panelist you cut off look good to the audience and feel good because it showed you were listening and valued what they said.

10. If there is a single big name or bestselling author on the panel, it is okay to allow them more speaking time than the rest of the panelists. Still make sure the others are heard from, even if it is to just react to the name's comments. After all, most of the audience is probably there to hear the bestselling author. They will feel cheated if they hear only a little from them. (See also our chapter on Panel Self-Defense.)

11. When possible, refer to scenes or ideas from a panelist's work. Gentle compliments such as "in your really exciting book, *I was a Teenage Stormtrooper*, you discuss how puberty affects judgement. Does this affect dragons?" This sets a positive tone and makes the author comfortable answering.

12. Always be sure to have a watch or phone with a clock. While the con staff may notify you that there are five minutes left, this is not enough time for questions from the audience. Depending on the nature of the panel's general topic, a good rule of thumb is to allow the last ten to fifteen minutes of any panel for audience comments. If a panel is one like those on world-building, writing hints, or game design, you may want to state at the start that you will try to take questions all through the panel. Then pause at natural breaks in the flow. If there are no questions, ask one of the questions you've prepared in advance ("what are some of the books you think do this well?") and let the panel respond to their answers. This will get the questions flowing. You may also ask the audience as a whole open questions, too.

13. Disruptions do happen. It's a good idea to ask everyone to silence their cell phones so a tinny version of "Play that Funky Music, White Boy" doesn't interrupt a passionate discussion of star drives. Babies may burst out crying. If the parents don't take the child outside on their own, a sympathetic glance and a gentle comment might urge them out the door. If other audience members start their own discussion in the back of the room, invite them to continue their private talk outside. Don't worry that they'll be upset about you drawing attention to them; they couldn't have been interested in the panel or they would have been listening. The occasional murmur between

Pros and Cons

seatmates is not a problem; an outright conversation doesn't belong in a panel room. If someone is insulting or too disruptive, ask them to be quiet. If they won't be quiet, ask them to please leave. If they cause a problem that endangers you or another attendee, call security.

14. You are a "moderator," so if things get too hot on the panel, try to make them more moderate. Do not let a situation escalate. There is no fame or pride in letting a feud start on your watch. Be positive; do not take a side if the dispute gets adamant. Rarely is a firm hand called for, but if name calling or other trouble begins, you are the authority on hand. Remind the panelists that the fans are there for the topic. Disagreements are excellent; challenges and insults are not. If a panelist is ranting or has an axe to grind, remind them as gently or firmly as needed that topic is not the panel's purpose.

15. If two panelists begin to challenge each other, it is your job to disarm the situation before the above happens. This may just need a word or two. If this disagreement continues, use your moderating authority to declare that item finished. Instead, ask a different question, and involve the whole panel. Change the topic. If possible, use gentle humor to interrupt the building tension then move on. Talk-show host Dick Cavett may have used the perfect argument interrupter decades ago when William Buckley and Norman Mailer began frothing at each other on his late night show. He observed to them

that it appeared that the discussion was "shedding more heat than light" on the topic. It embarrassed them enough (on live television) to stop arguing and go back to the discussion, at least for a few minutes. Warning: Do not break up a verbal fight by making them both madder at you than they already are at each other.

16. If you perceive a factual mistake in something a panelist says, phrase the correction as a question. By asking instead of making a blunt statement, you make it a part of the discussion and not a challenge to the author's expertise. Make it sound as if they are enlightening you, even by agreeing they were wrong. Let them talk. Don't use negative terms like "wrong" and "mistake." At most, say you had heard that fact defined differently and ask why that might be. Similarly, as moderator, do not disagree with a panelist who states a non-factual position. The best response is to ask the other panelists' opinions. If you as moderator disagree (unless the author speaking is close enough a friend), you embarrass them from a position of authority and challenge them as a pro. Let the flow of discussion correct misconceptions and errors.

17. If you know some members of the audience, use them to get questions started during the Q&A session. Ask them if they have any questions or for opinions of what has been discussed. They will forgive you for putting them on the spot. Use their first names when possible.

18. When time is nearly up, it's considerate to ask the

panelists for last comments, or to give them a chance to publicize their latest work. Remind them to tell the audience where those works can be obtained, such as Amazon, websites, or the dealers' room.
19. Always end by thanking the panelists, then the audience. Do not try to summarize what was discussed. If the audience claps, it is okay for you to do so while looking at the other writers as if to praise them. When the panel ends, compliment your fellow panelists on a good job.
20. Don't hang around afterwards and chat. This is best done in the hallway outside the panel room. Leave so that the next panel can get started. Urge all the authors to migrate outside with you if time is tight. Your job isn't finished until the room is cleared.

And finally, a few things to avoid:

Do not make, or let anyone else on the panel make, negative comments about the con you are at. Don't involve the attendees in your woes. It makes the audience feel uncomfortable, and your words will get back to the con-com.

Do not quote arguments or opinions from previous panels you have been on as a basis of discussion. Limit yourself to those of the panelists there.

Do not let the argument get personal. It is okay to call out a panelist for an inappropriate personal comment. Even if the panel is on sexual orientation or politics, insults are out of the discussion. Keep the argument on the subject, not on the participants. Quash *ad hominem* attacks.

Do not use the panel to push your personal opinions or grind your own axe.

If members of the audience leave before the end, do not comment on it. It's hardly ever a comment on the panel; most likely, they need to be somewhere else.

Do not leave the ringer active on your cell phone. It's embarrassing when your phone rings while you're trying to run a panel. In a crisis, send a text, but wait until you have asked someone else to answer a question.

Do not regularly text or check your email (really, we see it all the time). It is insulting to whomever is speaking at that time.

It is okay to sip water when not speaking. Even if you're starved, do not eat when on a panel. As the moderator, you should set an example of professionalism.

Don't embarrass your panelists. Do not call them by nicknames or sound too familiar with any of them, unless they are really old friends and the nicknames are in the public domain.

Don't fanboy/fangirl (for very long) if one of your fellow panelists is someone you admire. Try to limit gushing to a moment before the panel starts or after it ends. We all have the impulse. Restrain yourself.

Don't lose your positive tone. You set the mood for the panelists and audience.

BOOK SIGNINGS

o you are filling out a program participant questionnaire. You come to the line that asks, innocently enough, "Do you want an autograph session?"

The answer is yes. Yes, you do. If you are a published author, with even one e-book for sale, take the opportunity to do a signing. We include not only convention book signings, but during special events at libraries and other public venues, or after lectures or classes in which you are involved. If the event organizer has arranged for an autograph signing, make sure you get a seat. At the very worst, it will be one hour out of your life. At best, it will be a life-changing moment for you and your readers.

Why book signings?

To get your name out there among the reading public. Haven't the same people just seen you on a panel discussion? Not necessarily. They might be just passing by. Some won't have realized you were at the convention and are delighted to have the chance to meet you. Some might have come directly to the convention/event to have you sign and not wanted to listen to a lecture. This is a chance to do direct marketing of your work. (Panels, workshops and other appearances are indirect marketing.) SFWA Grand Master Gene Wolfe loves to do book signings. They make him feel good and gives him a chance to meet his readers.

Why do it?

To get your name out there. There are so many books for sale that a personal connection can earn you a lifelong reader. Like pros, all readers are different. Accept them all. Jody once had a man come up to her and brag that he had never bought a single book new. He had all her books but he bought them used. (This means no royalties and she never earned a cent on his reading her books.) She felt like telling him to get lost, but didn't. It would have changed absolutely nothing in the short run, and maybe lost her readers in the long run if he told the story to his friends.) OTOH, it is a chance for readers to come up to you. You may already have done panels and held other discussions and workshops, but this is a casual encounter, like an arranged date. You don't have a great deal of commitment to one another, but you and the reader can encounter one another under friendly circumstances.

How do you do it?

Publicize your appearance in advance. Make use of your website, Facebook page, blog, LiveJournal, or Twitter feed.

Your publisher may want you to notify them of your scheduled appearances so they can send you promotional material to use there or make sure books are on hand for you to sign. If you have an agent, give him/her a list of your appearances. Send out postcards or e-mail to your reader list.

You have the table between you and your readers, so don't be shy. If you need someone beside you to manage the crowd, bring a friend or relative, or let the con-com know you will want help. Be the same person you are on panels, but prepared to shake hands or bump fists. Don't go overboard. Above all, be professional. Smile. Make eye contact with the people who come up to the table. If they don't have any questions (or they freeze), make small talk. Admire a button they're wearing. Ask if they come to that convention every year. Engage them.

Make certain that you bring along a copy of your newest work, if nothing else. You should have a fifteen-word pitch that defines the plot for each of your books. Give readers a reason to look through the book. Scientists and marketing specialists have found that if a person touches an article, they are several times more likely to buy it. Let them touch the books. Answer questions, even ones that sound silly to you. Chat a little. Let them take pictures of you. Have business cards with your website and/or Facebook fan page, Twitter, LiveJournal address, etc. for them to take home. Any promotional item you hand out must have your name and website on it.

What if someone is rude to you or has never heard of you? Take it in stride. The former is exactly like a flamer in a chatroom. He's just trying to bolster his own ego. You're the one there signing your own published work. If someone hasn't heard of you, use your fifteen-word pitch. If they keep walking, well, not every contact is a sale.

If someone actually threatens you, call for security, *loudly*. That person does not belong at a convention and should have his or her badge yanked. If you are in a public place, scream for the police and call 911.

Most people will be respectful, and feel shy around someone who has done something they like. For us, this is the reward, getting to meet people who connect to us through our work. Relax and enjoy the experience. A little ego-boo goes a long way.

What do you need to have with you?

A pen. Not even that—a smile. Be welcoming to the readers. You can always borrow pens from them when you sign their books. Good conventions supply pens for the signing tables. Ideally, you should be self-sufficient. You will need a kit. What is in yours depends upon you. Romance author Jade Lee has a signing kit she keeps in every purse she owns. It contains pens, "Autographed by" stickers, business cards (or romance trading cards), sticky notes, either her own or her publisher's, a signature image (if you have one), breath mints, and the one thing Jade never goes to a signing without: lipstick. Bookplates are nice to have, but not necessary. The kit must be small enough to carry so you *will* have it when you need it. If an item you wish to have with you won't fit in the case, think hard as to whether it's necessary at your signing. Many authors keep a mailing list notebook. Others rely upon the reader using the URL they print on their business cards.

Should you sell your own books?

That depends. Can you count on a bookseller who will be at the event to have your titles in stock? Can you be certain that the bookseller will be informed that you are coming, and that s/he will have ordered your book in time? If not, you could print up signing cards or have other items readers can use as mementos. It's not as satisfying for you or the reader, but it's better than nothing. Because fantasy author Kathryn Sullivan writes for a small press, she often brings books that she puts on consignment with attending booksellers. In extremis, it is possible to buy a dealer's table to sell books when you are not engaged, but as Kathy points out, sitting at a table eats into your panel time and adds a further expense to your convention.

Many non-convention organizers will ask you in advance for your two or three most recent titles. The local Barnes & Noble will send a clerk with a few crates of books and a cash register. The perils of this arrangement are that you may sell only two of the ten copies ordered of each title. That means that the remaining eight (or so) are now at the mercy of the cover-rippers—Will they keep the signed books and put them on display, or send them back for credit?

On the other hand, carrying in your own book stock to guarantee availability means packing volumes into cartons or rollaboard luggage, making change, and deciding whether or not to accept dubious-looking checks. Thanks to technology such as Square, you can now take credit cards with a small device you attach to your smartphone.

For e-book authors, the world is changing rapidly. It is now possible for booksellers to load books onto e-readers on the spot by using a small and not very expensive device. (Look for these devices to appear at SF/Fantasy conventions first—we are, after all, the early adopters of technology.) In fact, that means that you the e-book author, will have unlimited stock available for the fans, whereas once a print author sells through the three copies of each hard-copy book said author has laboriously carried to the convention, that's the end of their point-of-purchase sales.

Timing

Face it, not every hour of every convention is ideal for an autograph session. Too early or late in the convention means a lot of people will miss you. Thursday or Friday sessions before the end of the working day will be lonely events. Mealtimes are deserts. Often, pleas to convention committees for better times will fall on deaf ears (sometimes even if you are the guest of honor). The ideal slots are post-lunch, pre-dinner on the main day of the con, usually Saturday. Those hours will be when the GoHs are scheduled, so there may not be room for you, but it can't hurt to ask.

In the interest of filling every hour, both con-coms and booksellers will want to schedule signings even during major events. Do not be inveigled into signing during the art auction, masquerade, special GoH events, the banquet, or,

God forbid, the Dragon Con parade. It's a waste of your time.

Some conventions schedule mass signings with every published author asked to participate. Those can be a lot of fun, but fraught with humility lessons. Jody's first mass signing at Worldcon in 1987 placed her at a round table with—noted here in reverse alphabetical order for dramatic purposes—Jerry Oltion, James and Alcestis Oberg, and Larry Niven. After the two people had Jody sign their copies of her first published book, she and the others got to watch Larry Niven sign books for an hour. (It was there Jody learned Jerry's useful acronym for authors like them, LKP, or Little Known Pros.) It is unavoidable that for at least a few conventions, you will be a LKP. It's a form of dues-paying, so accept it in good spirits. By watching popular authors, you will learn what to do and what not to do during signings. Don't be afraid to borrow a good idea, such as bringing a candy dish. (We recommend Jolly Ranchers. They don't melt in hot weather, they taste great, they are hygienically wrapped in cellophane, and people will usually take only one or two, instead of a handful of M&Ms or Jelly Bellys.)

Location

Autograph tables are often placed wherever the con-com can find room for three eight-foot tables in a row. Because of the way pocket program schedules are laid out, autographings are not always in the grid, which means readers—and you—will have to search the small print to find where they will be. In our experience, even otherwise considerate and longtime conventions sometimes stick the autograph tables in a hallway far from the rest of the event rooms. You might think it would be logical to put the authors in the dealers' room, not far from the booksellers, but tables there are profit-makers. The chance to sell three or more extra tables to hucksters usually outweighs logic and the wishes of authors to catch the attention of passersby. That also means that if a reader wants your latest book, s/he has to walk all the way back to the dealers' room, purchase it, and come back to your remote fastness for an autograph. Often enough, they won't consider it worth the trouble, and you won't see them again.

Foreign conventions

Don't trust your distributor to have your books. No matter how much they protest or promise that they will have them there, don't. Don't trust the local specialty bookstore to have your books. Really. Take it from our personal experience. Pack a dozen or so volumes in your suitcase. Even if you end up carrying most of them home again, you'll have given yourself more visibility. That's why you're there. This may be the only opportunity for someone who has vaguely heard of you or just seen you on a panel to buy your book. Distribution of American books in other countries is spotty and can be ridiculously expensive. (We saw *used* English-language paperback books for sale in Greece for $15.)

Who comes to book signings?

Average fans. Collectors. People who just want to meet someone famous. Booksellers. Some authors will autograph books for sale. We ask why not, when you already do it for bookstores? Some authors won't; respect their choice but make your own.

What about giveaways and other "premiums"?

Are they worth it? Kathryn Sullivan, who attends fourteen or fifteen conventions a year, has experimented with numerous giveaways. It's hard to find a convention attendee in the Midwest or at a Worldcon who hasn't picked up one of her pens or little flashlights with her name and book titles printed on them. After a good deal of trial and error, she has narrowed down her premiums to pens and advertising postcards (or bookmarks). She finds that readers come to associate her with the pens they find on the freebie table, and uses them as an icebreaker. "Just mentioning that the pens are free seems to make it okay for the person to come closer." Candy with the URL on the wrapper turned out to be a bad choice because it gets thrown away when the candy is eaten. Other authors have used appropriate premiums to create identity. A few years ago, John Ringo gave away camouflage-attired plastic ducks. National Pen, Café Press and Oriental Trading Company are good sources for giveaways.

Signing program books and autograph books

The blank page is the foe. Come up with something that helps fill the page a little. Some authors draw little pictures. Others have a rubber stamp. Terry Pratchett used to come to autograph sessions with an enormous rubber stamp of Death, and signed below the impression. At one convention Larry Niven used a rubber stamp in lieu of a hand signature. We haven't seen stickers or holographs yet, but why not? What will set you apart in a good way? Sign anything but a blank check. Many people have their own bookplates and/or blank stickers to put in the books at home they could not afford to carry to the convention with them. In this day and age of paying to check luggage on airlines, we sympathize.

What do you do if no one comes? Is that so horrible?

It feels horrible at the time, but we are assured by Alice Bentley, owner of the long lasting, but now shuttered The Stars Our Destination Bookstore, that many people want signed books but don't want to meet the author. She often had stacks of books to be autographed that had been pre-sold. For the author, though, it's yet another humility lesson. Sign the books at the bookseller booth on your way out of the convention. They will sell. You may even be asked to personalize them at a future event.

E-books—and e-readers

Many authors have already signed several e-book reader cases, and are delighted to have done so. The fan who asks you to autograph his or her e-reader is a devotee. Cherish them. There is only so much room on a Kindle case. If you are asked to occupy part of that space, the owner really, really wants you there. See permanent marker listed above.

Another thing you might do is print a giveaway card

that you can use if someone who reads your e-books has nothing to sign. Tom Knowles of Event Horizon E-Books supplies his authors with cover cards to give them something physical. Making that connection is why we are there, after all.

Conclusion

The difference between a good signing and a great signing can be as simple as whether you give away promotional material or sell a book. In any case, you have made a contact with a potential reader.

Make good use of your time behind the table. Even if no one stops to have you sign a book, smile at passersby. Always make sure that a potential reader associates you with a cheerful outlook. It will make them more likely to pick up one of your books than those written by someone who glowers. An autographing is only an opportunity if you use it as one.

Writer's Workshops

Do you love, I mean love, to read other people's manuscripts? Do you have the patience of a saint? Can you remain tactful even under extreme provocation? Are you considered a good teacher? Have you got a keen eye for what makes a good story? Do you have a great ear for dialogue? Can you explain how to make a plot work? Can you do it without imposing your own ideas? Do you adore trampling on the egos of others?

Scratch that last one. But if you answered yes to all the other questions, you may have what it takes to run a writer's workshop.

Adding to your value as a guest of a convention is vital to helping you stand out in the crowd of fellow attending professionals. One way in which you can do that is to offer to organize a workshop. Many up and coming writers attend conventions. They would relish the chance to have a professional such as you give them feedback. Why should you be the one to do it? It's a great way to give back to the community who, by the way, buy your books. Who knows? You may even be the one who gives that vital word of encouragement to the next star of the science fiction/fantasy galaxy.

You must understand up front that running a workshop is a lot of work. Depending on how you structure it, you will devote several hours to several days on organization and preparation. On the plus side, if you are good at it, this can give you a niche that will get you invited back to that convention year after year. There are so many aspiring writers out there who would love to have that resource available to them.

There are several formats currently used at multi-day conventions. In some, participants sign up ahead of time because of limits of space and the depth of attention that can be spent on each participant by the instructor(s). At many World Science Fiction Conventions, Adrienne Foster has run a well-known and respected workshop in which writers submit manuscripts up to a given word count ahead of time. These manuscripts are distributed to each of the participants and to the section moderator (usually including no more than four participants) and a panel of professionals for each session (also about three or four) for critique. In the session, a writer must listen to the critiques without comment until the end, to save time, then may ask for clarification or defend his/her work. This is a very successful model, giving good results to the participants, as each professional will have different perspectives on the work at hand. Variations are used in many other places, such as at Windycon in Chicago, under the aegis of Richard Chwedyk.

Another format is the single-teacher system. Barry B. Longyear, Todd McCaffrey, Ann Crispin, and I (Jody Lynn Nye) are among writers who run multi-day convention workshops on our own at larger conventions.

There are considerable numbers of variations on how a single teacher may organize a workshop. Participants may submit either short stories, the first part of a novel with synopsis, or a portion of a screenplay in advance. Those may then be distributed to the other participants for critique or just read and critiqued by the teacher.

Workshopping a story in the session is a valuable way for the participants to learn what works and what doesn't in their manuscripts. This can be accomplished by having all the stories available to read in advance, or have the writer read aloud from the work at the session (this latter in smaller groups only). Each participant weighs in on each story. One of the important things to remind them is that they will be in the hot seat sooner or later, and to follow the golden rule. Do unto others as you would have them do unto you, lest you be well and truly done unto when your turn comes.

If you don't want to spend your entire convention concentrating on other people's writing, perhaps you can run a small two- or three-hour workshop on one of your specialist subjects. The late great Hal Clement ran wonderful seminars on world-building. David Gerrold offers a workshop on developing characters. Allen Wold, a writer in the southeastern United States, has for many years run his two-part workshop on writing the narrative hook. Your preparation for a class like these would be much lighter. You would instruct your students in an exercise they would perform during the session.

If another writer at a convention is already running a workshop, does that knock you out of the running? Not necessarily. Dragon Con, Labor Day weekends in Atlanta, has several. For many years it has offered a two-day workshop that meets all day Thursday (before the con opens) and Friday. That one is limited enrollment, sign up and submit manuscripts in advance. The convention also features Mike Stackpole's a la carte workshop. Over the course of the con, he runs individual hours on specific topics. You can pay for one, several or all of them as you choose, no advance preparation required. There are also individual, specialty workshops.

Feel like giving a short seminar but organization is not your long suit? Many conventions have full writers tracks, such as Duckon (June, Naperville, IL) and Gen Con (August, Indianapolis, IN). Get in touch with the coordinator and pitch your idea. If it fits in well with the theme of the convention and scratches an itch it has, you may become an invited guest. There are also writer groups that meet outside of convention structures that might welcome you as a guest lecturer. I have done lectures and workshops at libraries, bookstores and other venues. The audiences may not all be interested in becoming science fiction or fantasy writers, but you can enrich their lives by the experience.

Many seminars and workshops are free, but some are paid. Much depends upon the expertise of and demand for the instructor, but also upon the convention's or group's finances, what resources are consumed, such as whether an extra function space needs to be rented. There's an old saying that people don't appreciate something that they get free, but you may not be in a position to demand money for your workshops early in your career. Still, whether or not you charge, you will earn the appreciation of the student writers for any guidance you can give them—all the more if you can really help them to become published.

Resources on how to teach writing classes abound. If you have not read *Techniques of the Selling Writer* by Dwight Swain (University of Oklahoma Press), you should. Todd McCaffrey recommends the *Save the Cat* books by Blake Snyder. While these are aimed at screenwriters, they help to explain plot points and pacing. SFWA.org has many informative files in its online archives. I also recommend you search out this useful article by the advice columnist Carolyn Hax (http://preview.tinyurl.com/7jsjnr9). In it, she gives advice to would-be agony aunts, but I think it also applies well to the job of teacher/critic. Don't forget the living resources of your fellow writers. All the organizations, including SFWA, Horror Writers of America, Romance Writers of America, SFF-FW, BroadUniverse, Novelists, Inc., the Authors Guild, and so on, are full of people who have been where you are now and can make intelligent recommendations.

Running a workshop can be a great deal of work, but it is also a lot of fun. I won't pretend you don't get ego-boo out of it, but there are more benefits than that. Many writers, me included, have discovered that you learn more about your subject when you teach it. So, get out there and share your talent. Your future favorite writers will be glad you did.

Attending Dragon Con

Conventions provide not only a great opportunity to promote your books and yourself, but also are a nearly unique opportunity to hear the comments and explore the attitudes of those who read the books we write. Upcoming columns will deal with various aspects of attending conventions as a professional author. Some articles will deal with the joys, hassles, and aspects of attending different types of conventions. Others, such as this one, will discuss one or more major conventions from the perspective of being an author who is attending it.

At this point we get specific and look at how to get the most out of very large conventions and, in particular, Dragon Con. Dragon Con is a large multi-media SF convention held every Labor Day weekend In Atlanta, Ga. It provides a good example of this increasing important type of convention. These also include many Comic and Anime cons which now include literary programming. The next article covers another distinct type of convention that also often has a literary section, gaming cons.

In attendance numbers among SF-oriented conventions, Dragon Con is second only to the San Diego Comic-Con, which has 300,000 members. Comic-Con is just down the road from Hollywood and the massive event reflects the proximity. Dragon Con, held over Labor Day weekend in Atlanta, GA, is a more general convention, less movie-oriented, less commercial and welcomes a wide range of fans. In excess of 70,000 fans gathered last Labor Day for the five-day convention.

In 2016, Dragon Con will celebrate its 30th year. What perhaps makes Dragon Con unique among the fan conventions of its size is that it is probably the most diverse, and in that lies your opportunities as well as concerns. Spread out over the six main hotels are major program sets that range from major TV and movie stars speaking and signing, to over twenty separate literature-related tracks, and from a near constant string of concerts to hundreds of paper, board and computer games. Last year on Saturday night there were seven simultaneous dress balls, some running until three in the morning. It's the only convention of which we know that has its own parade, complete with a grand marshal and marching bands. The sheer size and diversity of what the Chairman, Pat Henry, describes as being the "Mardi Gras for Nerds," presents every writer who attends with plenty of opportunities and challenges.

The greatest challenge, if you are not already a best-selling author or the USA Network is not featuring your vampire series, may simply be getting noticed. There are a lot of things happening constantly and at conflicting times. That means you will not often be the center of attention or may not even be recognized, no matter who you are. The convention is so large that you might never run into people who know you are there and are looking for you.

That said, this same diversity provides opportunities for some serious publicizing. Mike Resnick once expressed the problem and opportunity well. He observed that at most of the SF conventions he attends as a guest almost everyone there is already a reader and is likely familiar with his books and stories. He called this "preaching to the choir." While that is a good thing, it doesn't bring new readers into SF. Mike sees the real opportunity of Dragon Con as being able to "proselytize the masses." There are thousands of fans at Dragon Con whose interaction with SF is mostly watching television or reading comic books. Every one of those who meets you or hears you speak on a panel is a potential new reader who just might go out and buy all of your books.

A general benefit is that once you are accepted as a guest or professional, your name and sometimes bio are posted on the Dragon Con website, which gets tens of thousands of hits monthly. Like a bookstore signing, there is real value to you in the publicity for the appearance that goes beyond the value of the few books you help to sell. The convention also provides plenty of grist for you to tweet or blog about.

Perhaps the easiest thing is to look at each of the major areas of Dragon Con and how we have observed other authors benefiting from them. What categories do your books fall into? Contact the track directors and volunteer for their panels. Each track schedules its own speakers. During the show, look in the pocket guide and "The Daily Dragon" for more panels and meetings that interest you. They can also provide a last-minute way to both enjoy yourself and expand your readership.

The general literature and SF tracks feature the top names and editors in attendance. Even if you are not on a particular panel, asking good questions or making useful comments from the audience can get you noticed. It doesn't hurt to let the moderator know you are present. Being on the spot and participating also gives you a chance to speak afterwards with authors or editors on the panel which you might not otherwise get.

Look at last year's pocket guide or on the Dragon Con website and see what the specialty and fan tracks are. They range from British media to the Wheel of Time to Alternate History to Young Adult Literature. The directors of these tracks can be reached through the site as well. You may find fans among those who share your other interests.

There are a limited number of official signings available at Dragon Con. Even some special guest authors get only one signing or none. However, the dealer area and Exhibit Hall have numerous vendors you can contact, even during the show, who would be interested in having you sign at their tables.

There are almost 400 dealers in three large rooms. Don't limit your activity to just meeting the book dealers and signing at their tables. Game companies of all sizes buy booths, too. The small ones may not have a big budget, but many are always looking for good material to license. Is one of your titles or your series something they could sell a few thousand RPG supplements by featuring? Everyone wins when that happens. The larger game companies, computer and paper, are often looking for someone to write content. Finally, what else could your books inspire? Anne and Todd McCaffrey's Pern series has spawned the sale of tens of thousands of shoulder-riding, plush, leather or bronze dragonets.

Many companies demo or host their games in the Gaming Area. They and the thousands of gamers provide a great opportunity to meet and promote. Don't be reluctant to actually play a game that interests you. Certainly your teammates, and opponents, will remember the writer who played with them the next time they are in a bookstore.

Bring a few copies of your latest book. They are always appreciated and will come in handy for many of the opportunities listed above. It is good to have a lot of business cards as well. These tend to work better then bookmarks when making professional contacts. Make sure your cards have a valid e-mail address and telephone number. Don't crowd the rest of the space with data, but choose from your website, blog, Skype, LiveJournal, Twitter or Facebook info which of those you think would be the most effective point(s) of contact for professional use. You can always give someone more if they ask for it.

The Charity Auction is one of the best attended events at the convention. If you have some skill at auctioneering, volunteer. More easily, donate a few copies of your latest hardcover. When they are brought up for bid, you'll get your name mentioned.

Finally, it is traditional for most authors to sign books as they walk through the crowd. It never hurts to be seen doing this and it pleases the fans. If you are wearing a Guest or Pro badge, you are never really off-duty at a convention, so keep in mind the impression you make on meeting a fan. Unless you're late for a panel or a meeting (which they will understand), there's no need to blow someone off. Give them a little of your time. It can't hurt, and may make a fan for life.

The Saturday night banquet offers two opportunities for self-promotion and one for pure fannish enjoyment. The banquet features presentations to major media guests, including the Julie Award, named for the late editor of Superman comics, Julius Schwartz. In the last two years it was presented to Leonard Nimoy and Stan Lee. It's a great chance for you to see SF legends in person. Hundreds of fans attend for the same reason. For an author it is also a chance to sit down and become known by a tableful of fans or to mix with a tableful of writers and editors. Ask your editor if s/he has a table. Otherwise, sit down with some friendly people and introduce yourself.

Don't write off the "Walk of Fame." This is a large room of TV and movie actors who are signing their pictures for a small fee. Don't interrupt business, but if, for example, you based a character on one they played, or you feel they could star in the movie someone should make from your latest novel, give them a copy and your contact information. If they like your book, they may pass it on to their agent. Actors are people, too, and enjoy talking to professionals in other fields. Just remember how busy they can be.

One of the most amazing things at Dragon Con is the number of room parties on the three main nights of the convention. They are held in all the hotels, particularly the Hyatt and Marriott. Your badge ribbon as a pro or guest opens the door to almost all. Take a few hours and meet a few dozen fans. Chat with them and they will remember you. Many may well start reading the books of the author they talked to. (This works in the bar as well; at Dragon Con we call presiding over a table of drinkers the "Bob Asprin marketing program.") Many of these parties are thrown by SF clubs or other conventions. Make a point to get to those parties hosted by conventions from your home region or city. They provide a great opportunity to become a guest, or even occasionally a future GoH once the committee members get to meet and like you.

With over a hundred authors and editors in attendance, Dragon Con provides one of the better networking opportunities. Most of the book-related events take place in the Hyatt or the Westin hotels. Chat with your fellow panelists when the panel is over. Don't discount meeting the many comics writers, artists, and comic companies who attend and have tables. Would your book make a good comic or manga? Can you write the text for one? Do you need an artist to suggest for illustrations to your editor? Or to collaborate with you on a children's book?

Writers are not invited to Dragon Con, but rather apply. To become a special guest or professional guest complete the form available at DragonCon.org. Click on the Guest Application/Performance Submissions choice at the left side of the main screen to access it. The form is available beginning in December of every year. Your application is reviewed and a Letter of Agreement is sent for you to sign within a few weeks. If you do not get a response, there is a spot to drop a note to ask if it arrived listed under "contact us." In rare cases, the committee may even offer you one of the few complimentary hotel rooms. It doesn't hurt to let a track head in the area you write in know when you have sent in a form. April or May is not too late to send in a form for this year, though LoAs begin being issued in January. By

June, programming is being scheduled.

It is a good idea to reserve a room early, in fact, as soon as you can. A convention this size pretty much fills up every hotel in Atlanta all the way out to the airport. If all the official rooms are full, try the smaller Atlanta hotels. A comprehensive list is on the site as well. The Atlanta Metra light rail system runs from inside the airport to adjacent to the main hotels and is faster than a cab. If you drive, there is an open-air lot near the Hilton Hotel that is the closest economical parking option. Plenty of restaurants lie within walking range of the hotels, as well as two dozen fast food choices in the underground mall adjacent to the Hyatt. It's not a cheap convention to attend, but it can be worthwhile.

Finally, an exculpatory word or two: Bill made the mistake of offering to help with a problem involving authors and media guests at Dragon Con several years ago. Since then, his volunteer role continues and has expanded exponentially. Jody is also a regular at Dragon Con and beginning in 2011 has taught a writer's workshop there.

Attending Gen Con

So Gen Con has now grown into the second largest regular non-movie oriented SF and Fantasy themed convention in the USA, following only Dragon Con. The sheer size and nature of the convention provides many incentives and advantages for any author attending. In 2010 they had 30,000 unique visitors. Yes, it most certainly fills Indianapolis to bulging and all hotels within an hour. There is less emphasis on media than Dragon Con or San Diego since this is most certainly a gaming convention. In fact, by size and number of events, it is THE gaming convention. (The runner up being Origins, which is older and about a third its size.) Inside Gen Con there has been growing for 19 years a very good literary convention, the Writer's Symposium.

The Writer's Symposium and Beyond

One of the greatest appeals of Gen Con to any writer is the Writer's Symposium. For almost two decades Jean Rabe has been running this symposium, but starting next year it will be handled by Marc Tassin. We asked Marc to describe what this convention within a convention is:

"The Gen Con Writer's Symposium is a series of more than 80 panel discussions. The panels cover everything an author might want to learn about, from tips on crafting characters to world building to the business of writing. Most of the panelists are science-fiction, fantasy, and media tie-in authors, but the panels include writers of other genres as well, including romance and horror. This year, the Symposium even features a panel on writing screenplays hosted by an experienced screenwriter. There are also readings, informal question and answer sessions, and Read & Critique workshops. With events scheduled all day, every day, for the full four days of the convention, there is always something going on for writers."

Author's Alley

Beyond the Symposium is a somewhat unusual element known as the Author's Avenue. This is an area set aside by the convention where you can purchase a table at a reasonable cost (reasonable compared to other tables at Gen Con, at least) and sell your books off of them. This has some advantages, but because you have to purchase the table, not everyone can take advantage of it. Mike Stackpole, who has attended literally dozens of Gen Cons dating back to when the number was in single digits, observes of this area that it can be a great thing for promoting a new book or series.

Another good use for the Author's Alley is not selling books, but just promoting them. A number of authors have taken advantage of Gen Con's ability to let you reach thousands of readers from all over the country in one place. This provides a real range of opportunities for promotion and publicity beyond the normal panels and signings. Lawrence Connolly's sales have benefited from his Gen Con activities for much of his career. *"I started attending Gen Con when my publisher launched my novel* Veins *there in 2008. I was skeptical, but my editor assured me that the trip would be worth it ... the* Veins *launch was so successful that they've been having me do Gen Con launches ever since. I'll be back there this summer for the launch of my forthcoming horror collection* Voices.*"*

A Room Full of Hucksters

But the gaming nature of Gen Con is perhaps its greatest opportunity. As regular participant and Tekno editor John Helfers notes *"The foremost thing to remember is that Gen Con is primarily a gaming convention, so expect games of every shape, size, and variant you can think of. Writers should expect to be patient in trying to meet editors and other production staff, since they're usually pulled in about eight different directions at once."* Though he adds that some traditions can be found anywhere since *"the usual place to find other authors and editors—the bar—still holds true."*

There are over a hundred dealers, mostly game companies that have booths at Gen Con. Walking the dealer room is a must for any author. Not only can you mix with the fans, but there are business opportunities galore. Some are stores, whom you can encourage to offer your books. Many are small gaming companies, mostly offering role playing games or modules. They might be interested in creating a module from your current series. They also always need good writers. Writing for games can help supplement your income as it widens your audience. Gamers who enjoy your module may well go out and buy your books. Not only does Gen Con host a great marketing opportunity, but it also has a large concentration of potential other markets for your writing skill. Not to mention giving you the chance to write something that is both different and often great fun. You do not have to be an experienced gamer to write for a gaming company.

Who are these Gamers?

Gamers are readers. They have to be to able understand the often complicated loopholes, er rules, of the games they play. Mike Stackpole explains this convention's greatest attraction as *"Gen Con brings gamers and readers from all over the world, so it provides exposure to an audience that's huge. In marketing terms, they're a pre-qualified, target market, and they're primed to buy—and they do buy."* Simply put, all sixty thousand attendees are potential readers of your books. Something reinforced by the over twenty years of success the D&D™ novels have had.

The best way to start a conversation with any gamer is to simply ask them about the game they are playing or watching. If you don't interrupt their turn, the problem will likely not be getting them to talk, but you're getting a word in. Gaming is a hobby that is full of enthusiasm and at Gen Con you will see the most devoted gamers. Fortunately, with the possible exception of a few players huddled in the historical miniatures area, virtually every person there is likely to be a fantasy or science fiction reader. Those that aren't are easily interested. It takes a lot of reading ability just to master the loopholes, er rules, of the games.

Before You Go

If you plan to attend Gen Con, be sure to contact Marc Tassin so you can participate in the Writer's Symposium. Don't worry about fitting in, there are few communities more open and welcoming than gamers. As Lawrence Connolly has found, "You don't have to be a gamer to enjoy it. For my part, other than some work I did with White Wolf's World of Darkness series in the mid-90s, I am pretty much an outsider in the gaming universe. No matter. I never feel like an outsider at Gen Con." Once there just follow your instincts and enjoy yourself. Start conversations, go to parties, stop at booths and let them tell you about what they are doing and listen for opportunities in what they say.

One important observation from Elizabeth Vaughn, who has been attending Gen Con since before she sold her first book, is that "Gamers come in all shapes and sizes, but the thing you really need to know is that there are more women gamers than you realize. I think that by attending Gen Con I put my books in front of potential readers who wouldn't be caught dead in the romance section of their book store."

One warning—like most large conventions, Gen Con strains the local hotels to their limits. There are a surprising number, but only so many rooms within an hour drive of Indianapolis, Indiana. Lawrence Connolly warns that "a late registrant will likely have to settle for a motel in the suburbs. For the full Gen Con experience, you need to be downtown. Great restaurants and parties. This is one con that truly never sleeps!"

There are many great opportunities at Gen Con for both the new and established author. Mike Stackpole echoes many others we spoke to when he commented, "I've been attending since 1980, teaching there since the early 90s, and very happy with the exposure and networking opportunities the convention affords."

Shared Experiences

For the last several articles you have been given a ton of advice, dozens of warnings, read about a few convention memories and more than a few con horror stories. You might think that pros dread or fear conventions, when most writers look forward to and enjoy them. It is not fair for either the convention staff or potential attendees to paint what is an important outlet in such grim colors. Most things are done well. Incredible, fruitful, and downright fun opportunities exist for us at these events. We will end this collection by with some of the gathered good memories that come out of conventions. We asked a number of writers to send us some of their positive convention memories and experiences. These recollections turn out to be amazingly varied—but then, so are the conventions themselves.

You Just Met Who?

Most of us started out as avid readers of science fiction, not dreaming that we would one day be writers ourselves. One of the joys we have is meeting and getting to know the authors who wrote those books we hunted for on the shelves and pored over endlessly.

David Brin

Fave moments? Not as a pro but as a fanboy, getting to stand adoringly near C.J. Cherryh and Jack Williamson, learning how to treat fans right from Poul Anderson, who showed me how it's done with perfect patience, putting up with a gushing wannabe (me). And wallowing in the ideas spun off by fellow fans who constitute the smartest community of future-hungry geeks that ever set the tone for a better civilization.

Susan Sizemore

So, I'm a guest at Dragon Con, which supposedly makes me cool. But at least once a year I'll have a fangirl moment that totally blows my cool cred. One year it was when I was signing stock of my books at one of the bookseller booths. There was a man doing a book signing. I didn't pay much attention as I was in a hurry, had a plane to catch.... When I was done I turned around, saw the books the man was signing and yelled, "You're Peter S. Beagle!" Which, of course, he already knew. Another year, I was hawking books at the promo booth some of us authors had and a familiar person walked by. "Dave Tango!" (*Ghost Hunters* on SyFy) I yelled this time. He turned and came back and I gushed. I gave him one of my books. Cool thing was that he came back a few minutes later to say, "I know who you are" and ask for an autograph. Perhaps I should be embarrassed rather than pleased by my uncool gaffes, but I'm proud of being a fangirl too. I go to cons to show my true fan colors as well as be a pro.

Scott MacMillan

I must be the exception to the rule: I've never had a bad experience at a con, even when one con in Montana went broke mid-way thru the weekend (due to a heavy snowfall) and we had to help bail them out by agreeing to cover some of their hotel costs on our AmEx card. By the time the credit card bill arrived at home, so had their check. I doubt that would happen with a convention of baseball card collectors. Even if things *had* gone bad at some of the cons I've attended, it would still have been worth it. Where else but at a con could I have had late night drinks with Philip K. Dick, or chatted about silent movies with Lloyd Kaufman (of Troma Films fame), or ended up under a piano at a party at the home of Forrest Ackerman? Come to think of it, the con where I ended up at Forrest's place might not have been the best con ever ... but, hey! it was a helluva party! And that's what cons are all about. Some, like Dragon Con, combine the world series of people watching with panels that range from light hearted to the downright serious. Cons are a party that range from an intellectual feast to a hedonistic orgy of fandom, and well they should be. Enjoy the con, folks.

Tom Kratman

I'd joined Baen's Bar in the late part of 2000. Come Spring, one of the barflies, Leon Jester, asked me if I were going to go to StellarCon. I wasn't, but Leon mentioned that John Ringo would have some advanced copies of *Gust Front* for sale.

Also, note here that, having written the books that eventually became *A Desert Called Peace*, *Carnifex*, *The Lotus Eaters*, and *The Amazon Legion*, at that time decidedly non-SF in theme, and having had zero luck in marketing them, I had given up on the whole writing thing.

So ... John and I ended up hitting it off like long lost brothers, with both of us telling army stories in the bar of the hotel. It was freaking bizarre. I am not normally an especially charming person, but this one night it is like the finger of God has touched me on the shoulder with the divine voice saying, "Be thou charming this night, if no other."

Jim Baen comes in and takes a seat between Ringo and I. I introduce myself, "Hi, I'm Tom Kratman. Yes, I write, but, no, I don't write science fiction. So relax; I won't try selling you a book under the table." Then I go back to my stories. I think the next one up was the Sergeant Coffee Story, which appears in M Day: "Train to standard, not to time, Sergeant Coffee; stick the malingering son of a bitch again."

So, Jim and John exchange glances, then get up for dinner. I stay behind and finish some story or other, with the intent of leaving thereafter. John comes back and asks, "Why don't you come along with us." "Nah, he doesn't know me. It would be awkward." "You don't understand. He sent me back to *get* you." "Oh." And that's how I ended up writing for Baen.

Joshua Bilmes

One of the most important things in this business is networking and serendipity. Conventions allow for both, and can be crucially important for authors looking to break into the business. Not all conventions are equally important to this task. World Fantasy might be the primary convention intended for networking on a grand scale. Worldcon might have as many pros in attendance as World Fantasy, but as a smaller percentage of the whole. A "relaxacon" with a limited number of author guests isn't going to help much at all. The bottom line to me: I met Brandon Sanderson for the first time at a Nebula Weekend. John Hemry aka Jack Campbell came to me with an offer on his first novel in part because we'd interacted at a Worldcon. I hung out with Peter V. Brett and Myke Cole at a Philcon years before they became actual JABberwocky clients. None of these things were planned; they happened because I and my clients-to-be just made the effort to be at a place where good things might happen that we might be able to take advantage of.

Darlene Bolesny

The following occurred at the Crescent City Con, held just outside New Orleans in 2003. Bob Asprin knew that he had a panel titled "How to Write Humor." He warned me ahead of time that he wanted to do something different with the panel. He would not tell me what he had in mind, but he asked me to please be certain to attend the panel and warned me that he planned to "use me" as part of the panel. (Uh, oh....)

I sat near the front. He began the panel as I had heard him do countless times before—speaking about how pacing is important in writing humor and how humor is often an exaggeration of what would otherwise be considered normal.

"And what's more normal than a panel at a con, right?" he asked the audience.

He pointed to one of the female fans in the audience. "You, you're the 'Lady with a Cause.' I don't care what the cause is, but you have a 'cause' that you are championing."

He pointed to one of the male fans, "You're a new author. One book out. You are excited to be at your first con as a guest. But all you really want is to get laid."

Of course, this elicited laughter from the audience.

He pointed to several others and assigned their roles, and pointed to me and said, "You are the established, jaded author. You've probably seen more conventions than the rest put together."

Finally, he pointed to a fan in the audience and said, "And you are really from the IRS. You are tracking the jaded author trying to catch her claiming deductions she shouldn't be claiming."

"Alright! Everyone up front."

So we all dutifully took our positions at the front table and Bob started it off by having us do "introductions." I was at the far end of the table and when my turn came, I announced in as bored a voice as I could muster, "Hi. My name is Ann Rice. I write books." I chose Ann Rice as I had been mistaken for her a few times in the French Quarter. This, in and of itself, was not all that funny, but the audience certainly thought so. After the panel was over I learned that at the "Meet the Guests" affair held the prior evening and which I had come to late, none other than Larry Niven had introduced himself with the same phrase. "Hi. My name is Larry Niven. I write books."

The panel continued, with everyone playing their exaggerated roles to a *T*. The woman with a cause was angered at the killing of baby seals. The "IRS man" kept trying to ask leading questions. The new author kept dropping his hotel room number. Meanwhile, I can see Bob, at the back of the room, leaning against the wall with his arms crossed and that classic Bob Asprin smile on his face. He had successfully foisted the entire "How to Write Humor" panel off on the fans and myself and we were truly teaching by example—while he did nothing.

The audience was getting into it full swing by this time, and were asking their own outlandish questions—think the worst questions you've ever been asked on a panel. New people were now also crowding into the room, but the newcomers had no idea this was a "fake" panel! Finally, as the panel was coming to a close, Bob stepped back up and added the flourishing touches about how this was how an exaggeration of "normal" affairs could be turned into humor.

The panel became the talk of the convention. Between those who had participated, those who had wandered in late and thought it was real, and even the very good natured Larry Niven, who also came into the panel near the end, it had been a huge success. For weeks afterwards, fans I knew talked about it.

David Gerrold

In 1973, I was invited to one of the very first *Star Trek* conventions. It was held in February in New York at the Commodore Hotel, right next to Grand Central station. I had no idea what to expect, but it was a fan-run convention, so it was enthusiastic and high-spirited and joyous.

I remember several moments from that convention vividly, but two stand out in memory.

The first was an afternoon panel on writing science fiction.

It was still the beginning of my career, I'd only published one or two books, and I hadn't been to a lot of conventions, so this was one of the first times I'd ever been asked to be on a panel. I was the first to arrive and I sat down at the table. A minute later, Isaac Asimov walked in and sat down on my left side. And then right after that, Hal Clement came in and sat down on my right side. I was sitting between two of the elder gods of science fiction. I had grown up with their books and I was still in awe of both of them. On one side of me was *Caves of Steel* and *I, Robot* and *The End of Eternity*. On the other side was *Mission of Gravity* and *Needle*. And here I was, in the middle ... with um ... not a lot in print yet.

The little voice on the right side of my brain said, "What the hell are you doing, sitting between Isaac Asimov and Hal Clement?"

And the little voice on the left side of my brain said, "Better keep your mouth shut or the audience will be asking the same question."

Unfortunately, this was a *Star Trek* convention and I was the only *Star Trek* writer on the panel so the first question from the audience came to me. A young fan asked, "How important is scientific accuracy?"

I said, "I think it's very important. If I don't know something, I pick up the phone and call Isaac. And if he doesn't know, he calls Hal. So let me give the microphone to Hal Clement." Which I did.

The second moment was the banquet held on Saturday night. There was a live orchestra on the balcony overlooking the main floor, and as we all filed in, they began playing the theme from *Star Trek*. I don't think any of us had ever heard it played by a live orchestra before and the emotional impact was immediate. People just stopped and looked at each other and grinned in pure appreciation of the moment.

And one more very special convention memory. This happened at one of the last Worldcons Robert A. Heinlein ever attended. He was wandering around the dealer's room, browsing—and curiously, nobody was bothering him at the moment. He saw me and called me over. He was wearing that incredibly loud multi-colored coat he sometimes wore to fannish events. He said, "David, I have a story idea for you." My ears perked up. He leaned over conspiratorially. "Boy. Meets. Girl." And then he laughed heartily. I said, "Well, then it's only fair that I give you a story idea." I paused for effect. "The man ... who learned better." This time he laughed even louder. He was a very joyous man.

Jody Lynn Nye & Bill Fawcett

Just Plain Fun

There are a lot of satisfactions to be found at conventions. One of them is that unlike in our ordinary lives, the people think like us and often play like us.

Joe Haldeman

My best day at any Worldcon, predictably, was the day I won my first Hugo, for *The Forever War*, in 1975. I sort of walked around in a daze until some drunk fan pushed me into the swimming pool—wearing the new three-piece suit I'd bought for the occasion. By way of apology, he said I could hit him as hard as I wanted. Yeah, sure.

A wonderful night, nevertheless.

The most fun I ever had in a convention bar was at a ChamBanaCon, in Champaign-Urbana, in the seventies. There'd been a huge blizzard and everybody was stuck in the hotel for an extra day while the roads were cleared.

Andy Offutt had given a talk that included the advice that you could tell a good bartender from a bad one by making up the name of a drink that didn't exist—the Spayed Gerbil. A bad bartender will just shake up a bunch of reagents, and if you say "This is not a Spayed Gerbil," he'll just shrug and say "That's the way we make them here."

So about a dozen of us were down in the bar watching it snow, and when the waitress took orders, Mike Glicksohn asked for a Spayed Gerbil. She passed that on to the bartender—who was honest, and came over and asked how you made that drink. Mike said "He knows," and pointed at me.

I improvised on the basic pattern of a Negroni, but a big one—something like two ounces of Gordon's gin, one ounce of Campari, one ounce of red vermouth, and a triple shake of bitters. Add the juice of half a lime, shake well with ice, and strain into a huge martini glass.

They, or we, ordered ten of them, and then ten more, and so forth, the barmaid having to go mushing out twice for more Campari. The collective hangover the next day was legendary.

For some months the Spayed Gerbil was a favorite drink in Midwestern fannish circles. I suppose a lot of liquor cabinets in Illinois and Iowa still have a half-finished bottle of Campari gathering dust.

Carole Nelson Douglas

Among the mystery conventions, Malice Domestic in Bethesda, MD, is the most fun. The creative programming includes a "speed-pitching" breakfast where author teams change tables every couple minutes; an elaborate closing tea with British-royals-level hats; authors dressed as their characters; skits and, in the past, live radio mystery plays. The programming is always creative.

I was really charmed when I was Guest of Honor at CONduit 21 in Salt Lake City last year. It had a real "family" feel to it. I was treated like royalty and I had a fun live radio interview from the convention. The hotel room gift basket was full of fun and thoughtful survival-oriented goodies. And the organizers worked with me to do some offbeat sessions, like an interview where I "morphed" into the personalities (with costume bits) of three of my protagonists.

I gotta say the most fun I've had at any cons lately has been at the Dragon Con banquets. It's great to hear and see the award winners, who are giants in their fields like Leonard Nimoy and Stan Lee and Sherrilyn Kenyon and numerous others, and the entertainment has been prime, from world-class filkers to James Darren (who's still got the pipes in prime working order).

Jean Rabe

My best convention memory goes back a lot of years. I was running the Role Playing Game Association Network for TSR, Inc. (the then producers of Dungeons & Dragons), and I made a lot of appearances at conventions across the country. One such trip took me to Austin, Texas, for a lovely event put on by G.O.A.T. (Gamers of Austin Texas).

The con organizer's wife worked at a school for the deaf, and was aware that I knew American Sign Language. I wasn't totally fluent, but I knew enough to get me by in a reasonable conversation. And I could finger-spell my way through rough spots. Said lady also knew a group of deaf gamers from the school.

They were kids, I think the oldest was twelve or thirteen, and they were bussed to the convention so a "celebrity" could run a Dungeons & Dragons game just for them. The translator disappeared ... and left me alone with six wholly deaf children. I'd only ever "talked" to one deaf person at a time before. I had six of them in front of me, and they were all signing at the same time. My head started pounding.

The game began, an adventure I made up on the spot, as I'd not had any warning about this special sign-language D&D session. Good thing the kids all brought characters and dice.

It was bits of everything ... role-playing, a wilderness trek that featured gnolls from that Forgotten Realms novel I'd written, and then a crawl through some ruins. For more than four hours I entertained them, signing until my fingers and hands felt numb, and all the while answering questions I found difficult to put signs to.

"What does the dragon sound like?" a girl asked. Of course I'd put a dragon in the ruins.

It was the toughest D&D game I ever ran.

And in many respects it was probably the best ... and one of my fondest-ever convention memories. I talked about my novel without speaking words, got an idea for a deaf character, learned fantasy and science fiction signs I'd not been taught in my college sign language course, and had quite an audience through all of it. The other tables of gamers scattered around us ... they were all watching our adventure, the only sound coming from our session was the dice rolling.

And after these many years I still remember the "sign" for dragon.

Because SF Con People Are Special

What makes a convention memorable is almost always the people. This means not only the committee and volunteers (and thanks again to you all!), but especially the fans, who can be kind, generous, and understanding, as well as delivering restorative injections of ego-boo. They make a bad time better and create some of the most lasting memories for us writers.

Katherine Kurtz

One of my most memorable positive con experiences would have to be the LibertyCon a few years back, in Chattanooga, where, knowing how I do love ice cream, they laid on an ice cream social for me. What they didn't know was that I am a big David Weber fan, and he turned out to be a fellow Guest of Honor! How cool is that? Had a great time!

Janny Wurts

People who go to SF/F conventions are totally wonderful human beings—here's just how wonderful. I was at Dragon Con and ran off to a panel with a little black pouch on a neck string stuffed into a small portfolio bag I carry with me. I shoved the bag under the table at the panel, and in the course of pulling something out, the bag fell out onto the floor. It was dark on the stage, with a dark floor, and when I picked up to leave, I didn't notice I'd lost the pouch. The pouch had no identification, no name, not even a business card. It had a San Diego Comic-Con logo on it, and a pen, also with the San Diego Comic insignia, and close to three hundred dollars in cash, taken in at my dealer's table, that I'd had no time to secure. Needless to say, I discovered the pouch missing, and ran back, only to find the next panel in progress, and of course it was gone. Not being the sort to give in, I reported the loss to the convention committee's programming chair and amazingly, someone had turned the pouch in, cash intact, even though whoever found it could have no idea whose it was. This is honesty and integrity above and beyond the call, and makes me incredibly grateful to be a part of a community of people who are sterling characters in every way.

Don Maitz

I am happy to truthfully say my relationships with conventions have all been positive, and if there were any issues of note, they were not generated by a convention, their staff, or attendees who all have treated me exceptionally well. My own actions have been the source of any bumps that have come my way in attending conventions for over 30 years. I recently had an email from a west coast publisher and fan of illustration where I said I wished we had met. He said we did. He then reminded me it was he that returned my wallet, lost at the last day of a con in San Jose, CA. I did not know it was missing and I would have been in big trouble trying to fly home without it.

I hesitate to bring up the paintings Janny and I lost which were shipped to the World Fantasy Convention in Baltimore, but the positive reaction by the convention membership to pass a hat generating the money to register the missing works with an international lost art organization was so very touching. This is just one instance of a common thread. We are not alone in receiving the grace and big hearts of the convention going population and not enough can be said of the charity work they perform for groups in need. There is also the Heinlein-initiated Blood Drives that have been a source of life-giving generosity that have been donated by convention going fans for many years.

Jack McDevitt

Rather than focus on a specific convention, I'd like to make a general observation. I've never been to a con I haven't enjoyed. Sure, sometimes things go wrong. Sometimes you're on a panel in a room next to a place that is rocking with music and noise and you can't get over the racket. Sometimes you receive a schedule that is screwed up and when you get to the con you discover you had an assignment on Friday after all. Sometimes the panel topics need serious help. (And sometimes the guests make a mess of things.)

But the reality is that the staff inevitably tries hard to make everything right. And the attendees engage with enthusiasm. It doesn't seem to matter whether the con is in Boston or San Diego or on an island somewhere, it feels as if the same people show up. They have imagination and energy and sometimes they wear funny hats and they always make me feel at home. Maybe we don't always notice because we wouldn't expect anything less from a science fiction crowd.

Mel White

For me, the best part of conventions was—and still is—the energy I get from sitting down with friends, fans, and peers. Life has a way of wearing you down and wearing you out until your writing and music and art turn into a gray grind that you do simply because you've got to make money. And then you hit a convention.

Conventions are like a magical jam session, where everyone hauls out the old standards and turn them into play. Jokes on panels inspire art, music, writing, poetry—coffee and con-suite conversations turn into sparkling plot twists and interesting character development. Play turns into collaborations and opportunities and I come home from conventions feeling energized and ready to tackle any sixteen universes full of Dark Demonic Forces that you'd care to throw at me.

Toni Weisskopf

Several conventions have done this, including in recent memory the Seattle NASFIC in 2005 and in Orlando Oasis, which is to assign me, as one of their guests of honor, a highly competent local guide or liaison. I am the epitome of fan-to-pro, and very comfortable at conventions, but it just makes things easier when going to a part of the country that's new to have someone to show you the ropes. Other conventions that do this include Balticon, Boskone & ConStellation in Huntsville, Alabama.

Todd McCaffrey

My first science fiction convention was way back in 1968 at Lunacon. Charlie Brown was just launching *Locus*, Harlan Ellison still had jet black hair and could do Marine push-ups, and I was lost in a bewildering sea of introductions (I was all of twelve). TorCon, the Canadian NASFIC in 1970, was the second SF convention I recall and what struck me most was the hilarity of the panels with Isaac Asimov and Anne

McCaffrey. We should hope for a duo like that again in our lifetimes—they were amazing.

After that for the next many years I was going to English and European conventions, starting with Woostercon in 1971. That was the convention where we had the great paper airplane contest—we were all good and cleaned up immediately afterwards. Mum (Anne McCaffrey) was a great hit and got along famously with Brian Aldiss, Harry Harrison, and James "Jim" White, famous for many things including his "The Bermondsey Triangle" speech.

I think there's a magic to a good convention. Certainly organization helps but a good convention seems to rise above just mere good organization—perhaps it's the ability to adjust to the unexpected that makes a good convention great. Whatever it is, the best conventions are almost universally agreed to be *great* conventions even before they're over.

HeliCon 1993 in Jersey (on the Channel Islands) was one of the great conventions not just for the guests and the hotel but also for the incredibly good food available (including the chocolate shop in the hotel).

Aggiecons, both on and off campus, seem to reliably be marvelous conventions. Ad-Astra also seems to be charmed.

I'm convinced that a lot of what makes a good convention great is the committee and staff. Not only their level of experience but their level of enthusiasm for what they're doing. A convention run by people who *want* to run a convention is always a much happier place than a convention run by those just going through the numbers.

Dragon Con was an eye-opener when I first went. It's a large con, usually larger than the Worldcon, and more media oriented but not so much as Comic-Con has become. The large crowds, the hall costumes, and the level of excitement all add their own aura to the convention which makes it quite special.

Comic-Con is an experience by itself. You can find yourself in a human traffic jam on the exhibitor's floor—something truly terrifying to the claustrophobic (or even the remotely sane).

I think the real reason for a writer to come to a convention is to recharge the psychic batteries, to connect with the people who are a special subset of your readers. Come to have fun, come to be engaged in thought-provoking conversations and most conventions will exceed your wildest dreams.

C.J. Cherryh

Our best time was one everybody at Conquest KC in the old Hojo venue on a certain Last Day of the Con might remember: we took the whole hotel, and that included the bar, who served only fans, and sold a lot of their cheapest alcohol that weekend. Mind, this was in the days of fandom in which manners mattered, and if popcorn spilled on the con-suite floor, everybody including the GOHs got down on hands and knees and picked it up ... we operated under the Leave It Better than You Found It rule of hiking or conning.

Came the breakup of the con, last day, and as people loaded cars and prepared to leave, we all created one of the "endlessly mutating" and "constantly expanding" tables in the bar and ran tabs. We got down to the very last, the people who'd put other people on their tabs [to pay off favor-points and such] and had quite a bar bill going, since we'd started about 1 PM and it was now into the afternoon.

We called to the bartender that we were ready to settle accounts and pay the tab. And his response was that we'd been great guests and drinks were all on the house.

Lovely people, from the World's Oldest Waitress in the coffee shop, to the Thoroughly Fannish bar ... the hotel had its problems, and nothing was the newest, but for warmth and heart and "glad to see you back!" attitude, I loved that place.

At the opposite end of the spectrum was the last OKon held in the Camelot in Tulsa, which had some marvelous old woodwork, and castle turrets. It had been our hotel for many years, but it was changing hands, and nature conspired against that OKon. Not only did it rain, the swimming pool was lime Jell-O without any outside help but the rain—the a/c didn't work in most rooms, the carpets had rips, the sheets weren't that great, and nothing broke was getting fixed. Lightning hit near the pool, nearly electrocuting the GOH, who was near the pool's wrought iron fence. And as the con broke up and the last of us were getting our soggy baggage into our cars to go over to a post-convention dinner ... lightning struck the flagpole atop the tallest turret and took it out with a terrible crash.

All of us standing out in the parking lot agreed that God, as Convention Guest #0001, had just expressed His discontent with the Camelot management.

Someone Special

It isn't too surprising since those at a convention share an interest in SF that some of the people we meet there take on a special significance in our lives. I had to throw this one in early. Jody Lynn Nye and I (Bill here) met at a Capricon in Chicago one Sunday morning at 1:30 AM. We were married a little over two years later.

Brad Sinor

The funny thing is, when I mentioned that you wanted stories about good things that happened at conventions, my wife, Sue, said "Oh, are you going to tell them about how you sold your first book because of going to Dragon Con and meeting the publisher there?"

I smiled and said, "No, while that was a good thing, that was not the first thing that came to mind."

Back in the late 1980s I attended a science fiction convention in Oklahoma City called SoonerCon. That Saturday night I was asked to go out to dinner with a large group organized by my friends C.J. Cherryh and Jane Fancher. The restaurant did not have a big table where everyone could sit, so I ended up at a booth along with two guys from Kansas and a young lady I didn't know. "Hi, I'm Sue," she said, introducing herself.

I didn't know then but seventeen months later she and I would be getting married. We celebrated our 21st wedding anniversary last April. While I've had many good things related to writing happen to me at conventions over the years, meeting her was the best thing to ever happen to me.—Brad

I'd seen him on panels at other conventions and wasn't that impressed. I'm glad I was wrong. Brad's definitely correct; meeting at SoonerCon was the best thing that has happened to both of us.—Sue

SM Stirling

I met my wife-to-be, Janet, at a convention where I was semi-conscious due to staying up in the anime room all night watching replays of *Battleship Yamato* because I'd come out of the closet—literally; I'd been sleeping in a closet and the people I was crashing with gave it to someone else.

We *really* met at the World Fantasy in Ottawa, and conducted a long-distance romance. Finally, I got up the nerve to propose and headed off to World Fantasy in Memphis to do so. I was late; I burst into the panel she was attending; we kissed passionately ... and it turned out to be the "Sex in Fantasy" panel.

The writer who was chairing the panel pointed to us and exclaimed: "There! That's what we're talking about!"

Our 24th anniversary was this year ... and we still like to go to World Fantasy.

We couldn't have a much better ending than Steve just has.

SF conventions are most certainly a part of most writers' lives. If there is a pattern to all this, we believe that it is the people sharing their enthusiasm, generosity and energy that make conventions special not only for the readers and fans, but also for the writers other pros.

ABOUT THE AUTHORS

Jody Lynn Nye is a writer of fantasy and science fiction books and short stories.

Since 1987 she has published over 45 books and more than 150 short stories, including epic fantasies, contemporary humorous fantasy, humorous military science fiction, and edited three anthologies. She collaborated with Anne McCaffrey on a number of books, including the *New York Times* bestseller, *Crisis on Doona*. She also wrote eight books with Robert Asprin, and continues both of Asprin's *Myth-Adventures* series and *Dragons* series. Her newest series is the Lord Thomas Kinago adventures, the most recent of which is *Rhythm of the Imperium* (Baen Books), a humorous military SF novel. She also runs the two-day intensive writers' workshop at Dragon Con.

Her other recent books are *Myth-Fits* (Ace Books), *Wishing on a Star* (Arc Manor Press); an e-collection of cat stories, *Cats Triumphant!* (Event Horizon); *Dragons Run* (fourth in the Dragons series) and *Launch Pad*, an anthology of science fiction stories co-edited with Mike Brotherton

(WordFire). She is also happy to announce the reissue of her *Mythology* series and *Taylor's Ark* series from WordFire Publishing. Jody runs the two-day intensive writers' workshop at DragonCon, and she and her husband, Bill Fawcett, are the book reviewers for *Galaxy's Edge Magazine.*

After writing for the early issues of Dragon Magazine in the 1980s Bill Fawcett became one of the founders of and lead designer at Mayfair Games, a board and role play gaming company. He has continued his game design work creating a number of PC games and apps. Bill Fawcett & Associates has packaged over 350 books science fiction, fantasy, military, non-fiction, and licensed novels and series for major publishers.

As an author Bill has written or co-authored over a dozen books plus close to one hundred articles and short stories. Bill has collaborated on several science Fiction and mystery novels including The Guardians of the Three SF series, the Authorized Mycroft Holmes novels and the Madame Vernet Investigates mystery novels with Chelsea Quinn Yarbro. As an anthologist Bill has edited or co-edited over 40 SF anthologies.

Among the non-fiction books Bill has written are *Oval Office Oddities*, *100 Mistakes that Changed History* and *Trust Me, 100 Leadership Mistakes that Changed History*, *101 Stumbles in the March of History* and *Making Contact*, what to do if a UFA landed in your back yard. He has edited the Oral histories of the SEALs in Vietnam, *Hunters and Shooters* and *The Teams*. His historical "Mistakes" series take an often amused look at how the mistakes in history changed our lives include *It Seemed Like a good Idea, It Looked Good On Paper* (Engineering disasters) and *You Did What*. His military mistakes series include *How To Lose A Battle, How To Lose a War, How To Lose WWII, How To Lose a War at Sea,* and *How To Lose the American Civil War*.

IF YOU LIKED ...

If you liked *Pros and* Cons, you might also enjoy:

Million Dollar Professionalism for the Writer
by Kevin J. Anderson

Million Dollar Productivity
by Kevin J. Anderson

Million Dollar Book Signings
by David Farland

OTHER WORDFIRE PRESS TITLES BY JODY LYNN NYE

Mythology Series
Advanced Mythology
Higher Mythology
Mythology 101
Mythology Abroad

Taylor's Ark Series
Taylor's Ark
Medicine Show
Lady and the Tiger

Other Books
Launchpad
Strong Arm Tactics
Magic Touch
A Circle of Celebrations

Our list of other WordFire Press authors and titles is always growing. To find out more and to see our selection of titles, visit us at:

wordfirepress.com

www.ingramcontent.com/pod-product-compliance
Lightning Source LLC
Chambersburg PA
CBHW020257030426
42336CB00010B/811